Delaware

DELAWARE BY ROAD

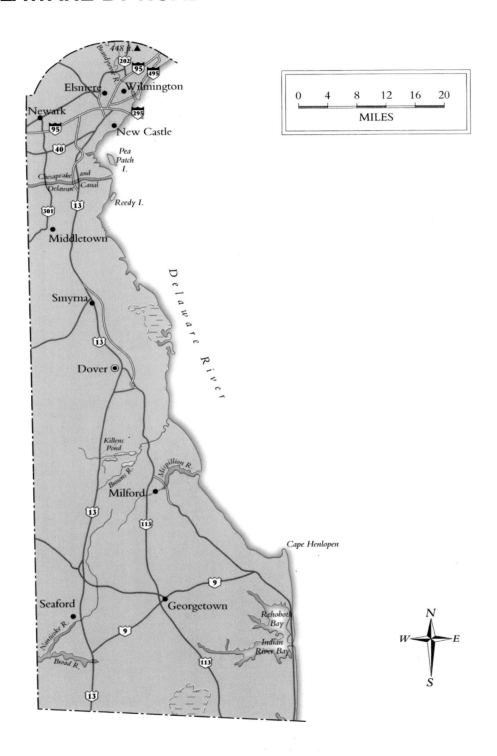

Celebrate the States

Delaware

Michael Schuman and Marlee Richards

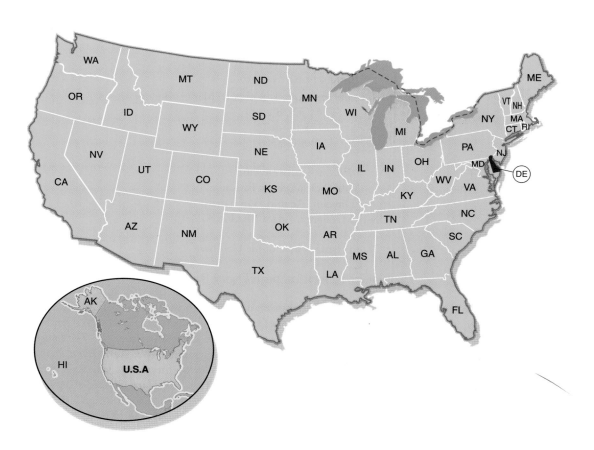

mc Marshall Cavendish
Benchmark
New York

To my friend Steve Otfinoski
—M. Schuman

Marshall Cavendish Benchmark
99 White Plains Road
Tarrytown, NY 10591-5502
www.marshallcavendish.us

All Internet addresses were correct and accurate at the time of printing.
Library of Congress Cataloging-in-Publication Data
Schuman, Michael.
Delaware / by Michael Schuman and Marlee Richards.—2nd ed.
p. cm. — (Celebrate the states)
Summary: "Provides comprehensive information on the geography, history, wildlife, governmental
structure, economy, cultural diversity, peoples, religion, and landmarks of
Delaware"—Provided by publisher.
Includes bibliographical references and index.
ISBN 978-0-7614-3399-6
1. Delaware—Juvenile literature. I. Richards, Marlee. II. Title.
F164.3.S38 2009
975.1—dc22
2008005369

Editor: Christine Florie
Publisher: Michelle Bisson
Art Director: Anahid Hamparian
Series Designer: Adam Mietlowski

Photo research by Connie Gardner

Cover photo by John Hartman/Digital Railroad

The photographs in this book are used by permission and through the courtesy of: *Superstock:*
back cover, 29; age fotostock, 113(T), 123; Michael Gadomski, 137; *Digital Rialroad:* Tom H.
Payne, 8; Tyler Campbell, 12; Rob Crandall, 56; Joe Sohm, 59; Julia Robertson, 83; *The Image
Works:* Mary Evans Picture Library, 33, 43; David Wells, 79; Mary Katz, 109; *NorthWind Picutre
Archive:* 34, 36, 37; *Getty Images:* Hulton Archive, 42, 127; Will McIntyre, 81; Jake Rajs, 85;
Dan Callister, 129; Paul Kane, 132; *Jupiter Images:* Steve Cohen, 62; *Mark Gibson:* 68, 99;
Corbis: Kelly-Mooney Photography, 11; Kevin Flemming, 15, 16, 54, 57, 63, 65, 67, 87, 89, 90,
92, 97, 102, 107, 121, 125; Ed Young, 22; Corbis, 48, 76; Bettmann, 50, 60; Mark E. Gibson,
52; Roman Soumar, 94; William Bake, 134; *Alamy:* Andre Jenny, 95; Janice Hezeldine, 96; Philip
Scalia, 100; *AP Photo:* Dan Gill, 19; Gary Emeigh, 23; Chris Gardner, 70,; Pat Crowe, 72; Jack
Shaum, 104; *The Granger Collection:* 26, 31, 46, 49, 105; *Minden Pictures:* Gerry Ellis, 20; Mike
Potts, 21; Stephen Dalton, 113 (B); *Dembinsky Photo Associates:* Dominique Braud, 117.

Printed in Malaysia
1 3 5 6 4 2

Contents

Delaware Is . . .

Delaware is a state with close borders filled with unusual treats . . .

Delaware "is like a diamond, diminutive, but having within it inherent value."

—John Lofland, poet, 1847

The land includes a "noble river and bay" that would become "a Jewel in the royal crown."

—early Swedish colonizer, 1650s

. . . where natural beauty extends from end to end.

"The scenic ponds created to supply energy to the dozens of grist and lumber mills are too perfect to be captured by mere artist or mere word. They have to be experienced firsthand."

—Judy Colbert, travel writer

Summer blooms with "open swamps that are showy flower gardens, high pinelands with several varieties of goldenrod coming into flower, ponds where water-lilies, spatterdocks, and floating-heart cover the surface—the edges surrounded with pickerel-weed and arrowhead."

—Dr. John Small, curator, New York Botanical Garden, 1929

Notable figures recognize this amazing state.

"As long as the country shall last, with pride by the citizens of Delaware—that she was the first to accept the glorious Union, in an hour of trials, of doubt, and of darkness; and I think that you may well proclaim that she will be the last to give it up."

—President Franklin Pierce, 1853

"Not only do I admire her [Delaware] for what she is, her devotion to the Constitution and the Union, but for the high rank which she has always sustained in the history of our country, for her statesman, her heroes, both on land and on the sea."

—General Winfield Scott, October 22, 1852

And even through troubled times . . .

"The Lenni-Lenape Indians, who were duped by both the white settlers and by rival tribesmen, and who retaliated with force and eventually became refugees of their own land."

—Benjamin Eisenstat, researcher, 1959

"Negro writers [in Delaware] have been obligated to have two faces. If they wished to succeed they have been obliged to satisfy two different audiences, the black and the white."

—Jay Saunders Redding, Wilmington author and educator, *To Make a Black Poet,* 1939

. . . Delawareans always work toward a brighter future.

"Getting to where Delaware State is today was a challenge, my friends—a challenge proudly met by the people of this community and the Delaware State family."

—Michael N. Castle, U.S. House of Representatives, Delaware

"We all know each other, and if there's a problem, we can bring the people and resources together to solve it. This is why I say Delaware is small enough to work."

—Pierre S. "Pete" du Pont, former governor

People from Delaware know that greatness comes in all sizes and forms. They see a state filled with sandy beaches, abundant waterways, and salty marshes. Rich farmland adds to the state's industry and invention, expanding its productive reach across local and national borders. Delawareans take pride in knowing that besides varied landforms their few cities sparkle with life. Towns teem with havens of local culture and state history. Delawareans like to say that rather than small, their state is a "small wonder." This is Delaware's special story.

Chapter One

Land of Small Wonders

Hundreds of millions of years ago, the land that became Delaware lay under ocean waters. Thick glaciers covering the earth froze and melted, lowering and raising the ocean. About 200 million years ago the melting glaciers caused the earth to shift. Underwater volcanoes erupted and pushed rocks above the water's surface. These rocks created the Appalachian Mountains. Northern Delaware formed at the base of the mountains.

The ocean floor continued to move over millions of years. Plates of rocks bumped into each other. Tides flowing in and out against the rock formations left layers of ground rock, clay, and sand extending from the mountains. This mixture provided the foundation for Delaware's flat plain.

About 12,000 years ago, the last glacier to the north melted. Sharp chunks of ice cut into the land, leaving a wide river and many channels for smaller rivers and streams. Thereafter, Delaware's two main landforms, mountains to the north and plains to the south, defined the area that would become the state.

The Brandywine River Valley is known for its rolling hills and natural beauty.

Today, most of the state's 1,982 square miles lies on the low, flat Atlantic Coastal Plain, on the eastern seaboard of the United States. The plain stretches from New Jersey in the north to Florida in the south. The northernmost tip of Delaware is the only corner of the state that is not part of the Atlantic Coastal Plain. This region makes up the Piedmont, an area known for rolling hills and peaceful valleys.

Because of its small size, Delaware is a difficult state for some travelers to locate on a map. The state seems lost along the Atlantic coast, tucked in between New Jersey and Maryland. Deborah Haskell, who is executive director of the Delaware Heritage Commission, says, "Some cynics call us 'Dela-where?'"

FINDING DELAWARE

So where is "Dela-where?" Delaware sits about halfway down the East Coast of the United States. The state occupies the northeastern part of a stretch of land known as the Delmarva Peninsula. The peninsula is a wide stretch of land bordered on three sides by water, in this case the Atlantic Ocean and Chesapeake Bay. The term *Delmarva* comes from names of the three states that share the same peninsula: Delaware, Maryland, and Virginia. To the west and south of Delaware is Maryland. Below Maryland on the peninsula is a skinny patch of land that belongs to Virginia.

Delaware borders two other states. The northern border with Pennsylvania is unusual: it hooks in a semicircle. The reason for the curved border goes back to battles between early settlers of New Jersey and Delaware over trade routes along the Delaware River. Repeated court cases, one as recent as 1934, awarded border rights to Delaware that reached 12 miles in all directions from the steeple of the New Castle courthouse. These rulings account for Delaware's official northern arc.

To Delaware's east is water. The Delaware River separates Delaware from New Jersey. As the river extends southward and widens, it becomes Delaware Bay. The bay spills into the Atlantic Ocean to the southeast.

Rafters paddle over gentle rapids of the 330-mile-long Delaware River.

Although some gentle hills rise in the north, Delaware is one of the flattest states in the nation. Its highest point, in New Castle County near the Pennsylvania state line, reaches only 442 feet above sea level. Oddly, the highest point in Delaware is lower than the lowest places in many American states.

The lowest elevation in Delaware is sea level along the coast. But the average altitude rises only about 60 feet above sea level. This level could be scary considering the recent, continuing extreme changes in the earth's weather. Storms and melting glaciers that flood and raise ocean waters pose a real threat to the state's very existence.

Unlike the gentle rolling hills of northern Delaware, most of the state is flat.

LAND AND WATER

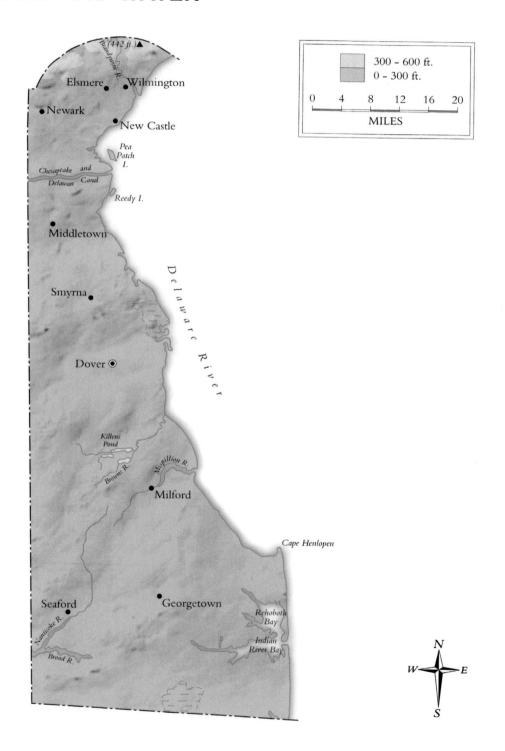

300 – 600 ft.
0 – 300 ft.

MILES
0   4   8   12   16   20

N
W   E
S

(442 ft.) ▲
Brandywine R.
Elsmere   Wilmington
Newark
New Castle
Pea
Patch
I.
Chesapeake   and
Delaware   Canal
Reedy I.
Middletown
Delaware River
Smyrna
Dover ◉
Killens
Pond
Browns R.
Mispillion R.
Milford
Cape Henlopen
Seaford   Georgetown
Rehoboth
Bay
Nanticoke R.
Indian
River Bay
Broad R.

Yet people who live here like the land where they live. Those looking for mountains drive to nearby Pennsylvania, Maryland, and Virginia. And Delaware has something that some states with huge mountains don't have: miles of warm, beautiful beaches.

MORE THAN SIZE

Delaware looks like an upside-down elf shoe, with the northern toe pointing eastward toward New Jersey. Its area of 1,982 square miles gives Delaware the rank of second smallest of the fifty states, behind Rhode Island.

At its longest point Delaware is just 96 miles long. That's less than one mile for every eight along the California coastline, which is roughly 800 miles long. At its widest point, Delaware stretches 35 miles across. For comparison, the distance that separates just two Texas cities, Dallas and Fort Worth, is 30 miles. The state of Texas, at its widest point, is almost 800 miles across, almost twenty-three times as wide as Delaware.

The people of Delaware are proud to live in a small state. "We're small, but we feel mighty. We don't feel small," says Deborah Haskell.

BAYS AND BEACHES

For such a small state, Delaware has a long shoreline: 381 miles. The Atlantic coastline reaches from Fenwick Island on the Maryland border to Cape Henlopen at the opening to the Delaware Bay. The Atlantic Ocean brushes and batters 28 miles of beach in southern Delaware. Delaware's beaches thrill vacationers with a wide, sandy coastline. A smattering of dunes hides inland amid nearby pine forests. The largest, the Great Dune at Cape Henlopen State Park, rises about 80 feet above the shoreline.

Delaware's coastline has wide, sandy beaches. This is the popular Rehoboth Beach.

Along much of the southern stretch of Delaware is a sandbar that separates the ocean from three bays: Little Assawoman Bay, Indian River Bay, and Rehoboth Bay.

Farther north along Delaware Bay, the shoreline has miles of inlets and coves. They provide havens for beaches, salt marshes, and national wildlife preserves.

Bombay Hook National Wildlife Refuge is the biggest of these preserves at almost 16,000 acres. It is home to gaggles of snow geese, many other waterfowl, and even a nesting pair of bald eagles. Maurice Barnhill, an avid bird-watcher, says, "If I had to pick a single area along the Middle Atlantic

Snow geese fly over the Bombay Hook National Wildlife Refuge.

region for bird-watching, Delaware would be the best. It's a small state, so the list [of birds seen] will not be as big as the lists of other states. But Delaware sits along the Atlantic flyway and it is absolutely superb for seeing shorebirds."

The state is also laced with streams and rivers. The most important is the Delaware River, which forms the New Jersey–Delaware border and empties into Delaware Bay. The largest river in Delaware is the Christina, a tributary of the Delaware River in the busy northern portion of the state. The bustling Port of Wilmington lies at the mouth of the Christina. Brandywine Creek also flows through northern Delaware and empties into the Christina River.

Small waterways crisscross the rest of the state. These include the Broadkill and Mispillion rivers in central Delaware. The St. Jones River runs through the state capital of Dover. While these three rivers all lead into Delaware Bay, the Nanticoke River in southwestern Delaware flows west through Maryland and into Chesapeake Bay.

GREAT CYPRESS SWAMP

One special body of water is the Great Cypress Swamp in south-central Delaware. It is the northernmost cypress swamp in the nation, named for the many bald cypress trees that dominate the region. The trunks of these trees, which flare out at the bottom, look like elephants' feet. One bald cypress, known as the Patriarch Tree, is thought to be the oldest tree in Delaware. It is 50 feet across and more than six hundred years old.

A green velvety carpet covers the swamp water each summer. Some visitors think it looks like green slime. The green actually comes from a plant called duckweed. In the fall the duckweed begins dying out, and the cypress needles turn cinnamon-red before falling off. According to naturalist Jenna Luckenbaugh, "The swamp is really nice for canoeing. You really feel like you're down in the Deep South."

WATER, WATER EVERYWHERE

Being surrounded by water should mean that water is in ready supply. But most water around Delaware is undrinkable: it's salt, rather than fresh, water. Worldwide, 70 percent of the earth's surface is made up of water, but just 1 percent is drinkable. A major problem particularly for coastal states, such as Delaware, is finding enough water for everyday activities. People usually need only a half-gallon of water per day. Yet, Delawareans average 75 to 100 gallons per person a day much like each person in the United States.

State lawmakers realized that the only way to prevent dangerous shortages would be to cut down on use of water. To encourage conservation, the state promoted a list of twelve ways citizens can reduce their need for water. Suggestions include everything from fixing leaky faucets and toilets to not letting water run while rinsing vegetables and dishes or brushing teeth and shaving.

THE WEATHER REPORT

Delaware's coast has a moderate climate. Ocean breezes cool the land in summer, and warm ocean waters of the northern Gulf Stream temper the winters. Shore temperatures may rise 10 degrees Fahrenheit higher in winter or 10 degrees lower in summer. Often the milder climate allows residents to enjoy summers that continue into late autumn. The average highest summer temperatures climb to between 81 and 86 °F. Meanwhile, average nighttime winter temperatures can drop to 22 to 28 °F, but warming during the day to 39 to 44 °F.

In summer, thousands of visitors escape muggy cities, such as Baltimore and Washington, D.C., to enjoy balmy days on the Delaware shore. Kevin and Linda Nielson leave their home in northern Virginia to vacation on Delaware's beaches. Kevin says, "We usually start going in mid-May.

It's still cool but if you have a day when the temperature gets into the high eighties, the water can really feel good. The beach season lasts well into September."

Inland weather can be more extreme. Summer air is often more hot and humid than along beaches. In winter, snow and sleet are common. New Castle County remains Delaware's snowiest region, with about 18 inches of snow a year. This amount seems high compared with about 12 inches along the coast, but it's low in relation to other coastal states. In total, Delaware averages about 46 inches of precipitation—rain, snow, and sleet—a year.

During the winter, Delaware receives its share of snow.

PLANTS AND ANIMALS

Delaware contains many varieties of furry creatures, large and small. Raccoons, foxes (both red and gray), opossums, rabbits, and white-tailed deer make their homes in Delaware's forests. Muskrats, mink, and otter thrive in the state's wetlands where they share space with a mix of mallard, mottled, wood, and pintail ducks.

Delaware's waterways play a major role in bird migration. From late May until mid-June, more than 1.5 million birds pass through areas such as the Bombay Hook National Wildlife Refuge. Bird lovers thrill at the sight of huge flocks of shorebirds—dunlins, stilts, dowagers, and vulture—that rest on their summer migration. They arrive from South America on their way north to breeding grounds in the Arctic.

Delaware provides a home or rest stop to more than 256 species of birds. About 80 percent of the nation's snow geese make their way along Delaware's Atlantic coast. The ocean and bay offer homes to shorebirds, such as egrets, ibises, and herons. Among the many birds living in the state are Canada geese, snow geese, bobwhite quail, red-winged blackbirds, and ring-necked pheasants.

Residing in Delaware's many waters are several kinds of frogs and turtles including bullfrogs, diamond-back terrapins, and snapping turtles.

Egrets are a common sight along Delaware's coastal marshes.

Ribbed mussels and fiddler crabs breed in the state's salt marshes. The state fish is the weakfish, which is also known as the sea trout, gray trout, or tiderunner. Other common saltwater fish include bluefish, sea bass, flounder, croakers, and porgy. Freshwater fish abundant in Delaware are bass, bluegill, perch, trout, crappie, and pickerel.

The largest population of horseshoe crabs in the world can be found in Delaware Bay. Thousands of crabs lay their eggs on the Delaware Bay shoreline during spring's high tide. The eggs provide food for the migrating birds.

Delaware, New York, Massachusetts, New Hampshire, and Tennessee all claim the same state bug—the ladybug. Other insects found buzzing through the summer air or lolling on leaves include crickets, fireflies, and praying mantises. Delaware also boasts the largest moths in North America. The greenish luna moth and the brownish red cecropia moth both have wingspans that can reach 6 inches.

Delaware once produced many wreaths commonly seen on doors during the holiday season. Now the state tree is the American holly. Other trees found in Delaware are sycamores, beeches, yellow poplars, hickories, and oaks. For flowers, delicate orchids thrive in Delaware's wetlands. Violets, American lotuses, and lady's slippers also grow in the wild here. Cattail and cordgrass bloom in salt marshes.

A mass spawning of horseshoe crabs takes place every year along Delaware's coast.

SOMETHING PEACHY

Delaware's state flower is the peach blossom. When it was adopted, in 1895, there were more than 800,000 peach trees growing in the state. Peaches were once so abundant that a 1915 hit song was titled "When It's Peach Picking Time in Delaware."

Peaches were not native to Delaware. Spanish explorers brought them to North America in the 1500s. By the 1600s so many peaches were grown in Delaware that many people fed them to their hogs as slop.

Into the nineteenth century, Delawareans shipped millions of baskets of peaches to distant markets by steamboat and train. Delaware peach production reached its peak in 1875, when growers exported more than 6 million baskets. For the next forty years, peach peddlers throughout the Mid-Atlantic states were heard chanting the singsong refrain, "Here's your peaches, your fine Delaware peaches, your sweet Delaware peaches."

In the 1890s disaster struck. A virus known as the peach yellows began ruining the state's peach industry. Many peach growers lost so much money that they burned their orchards and turned the land into pastures. Others began growing apples, melons, and strawberries instead of peaches. Before the virus hit in 1890, 5 million peach trees produced fruit in the state. By 1920 that number had dwindled to 500,000. Peaches are still grown in Delaware, but the fragrant fruit is no longer the top state crop.

SAVING DELAWARE'S ENVIRONMENT

Over the years, farms and suburban housing have replaced forests that once gave wildlife their habitats. Businesses and shopping centers increased as well, polluting wetlands and rivers and pushing out wild animals and plants. To some extent, most states have had to deal with these concerns. But Delaware has been a leader among eastern states in preserving land from overdevelopment. The state has worked with federal lawmakers to pass a series of laws that resulted in continued preservation of Delaware's natural resources. Legislators in Dover created a state system of parks, which help to preserve the shoreline. Yet, much needs to be done to protect Delaware's natural resources.

To encourage interest and action in environmental issues, Delaware established a program that celebrates students from three different age categories who act to "protect, restore, or enhance the state's natural resources."

Two high school students care for an organic garden near Middletown.

Winners of the Young Environmentalist Award have devised a variety of worthwhile projects. Two creative middle-school environmentalists developed a program to tell Cape Henlopen State Park visitors about the endangered piping plover bird. A high schooler studied erosion at Rehoboth Beach. Delaware believes that investing in programs for students will result in greater awareness and protection of the environment for years to come.

CHICKENS AND POLLUTION

Delaware also works with specific populations to improve and protect the environment. For example, southern Delaware is covered with farms, and poultry contributes to 70 percent of the state's farm income. Most of the soybeans and corn grown in the state goes to feeding chickens.

But chicken farming is responsible for problems unforeseen when the business began in the 1920s. Chicken manure, which farmers regularly use as fertilizer, is among the greatest polluters of southern Delaware's lakes and rivers. Rainwater carries nutrients from the fertilizer into Delaware's waterways, such as the Broadkill and the Mispillion rivers. Runoff from farms pollutes the water and harms plants and marine animals.

The Environmental Protection Agency (EPA), the government organization in charge of overseeing air and water quality in the United States, is trying to combat fertilizer pollution. It has announced a plan that would require Delaware's chicken farmers to get pollution-control permits to be able to conduct business. The farmers have been given a few years to find alternative ways of disposing of chicken manure before the permit requirement takes effect.

Most poultry farmers are not pleased with the EPA's plan. Kimberly Esham blasts it as "one more lousy thing we have to do just to make a living." A farmer named John C. Atkins insists that a few years is not enough time to find other ways of disposing of the chicken manure. Atkins says the EPA "is moving too fast. These environmentalists, if they shut this chicken industry down, maybe they can come down here and eat the beach sand. This whole industry has been here for seventy years. We're not going to clean it up overnight."

In 2006 the first major breakthrough occurred. A large poultry processing corporation that buys chickens from family farms reached an agreement with the EPA and the state of Delaware. The company agreed to restore and protect waters of Delmarva by working with local authorities to devise the best practices for poultry farms. Meanwhile, the state is researching alternative ways of disposing of the waste. One possibility is burning it to fuel power plants. Another is turning it into commercial fertilizer. A third is finding a treatment for chicken manure that will keep it from harming the water. Hopefully, these or other ideas will allow both Delaware's farmers and its environment to thrive.

Chapter Two
The First State

The first Europeans to reach present-day Delaware found the land already inhabited. For centuries, several clans of American Indians had resided throughout what became New Jersey, Pennsylvania, southern New York, and Delaware. The clans followed different leaders but shared many similar customs and traditions.

The two main Indian nations—the Lenni-Lenape and Nanticokes—and smaller clans of American Indians hunted, fished, and farmed along the plains and valleys. They spoke a form of the Algonquin language. They lived in dome-shaped longhouses held together by mud covered with grass, bark, and corn husks. Their traditions stayed alive through storytelling. And true to American-Indian custom, they had no tradition of owning land.

The Lenni-Lenape, which means "original or true people" in Algonquin, built small villages mainly along the banks of the Delaware River. Other Algonquin-speaking tribes in the region called the Lenape *grandfather* because they recognized their own origins in Lenape territory. In the Algonquin tradition, men and women had separate but equal roles. Men cleared the fields and broke the soil, women tended to the crops. The Lenape

In the 1600s the New Netherland *arrived with Delaware's first Dutch settlers.*

THE LEGEND OF SNOW BOY: A LENNI-LENAPE TALE

Winter storms were common in the Middle Atlantic states, including Delaware. So the Lenni-Lenape created several legends about winter. One such tale relates the story of Snow Boy.

According to ancient legend, when other children angered Snow Boy, he grabbed their hands and sucked on their fingers. To everyone's surprise, the wet fingers turned black and stiff. The fingers looked as if they had frozen from frigid weather.

One spring, when Snow Boy was old enough to go about on his own, he decided to leave home. Before he left, he told the villagers that he had great powers and had been sent to Earth to help people track other creatures. He said he would return often, but not in human form. When snow fell, people would know that he had come visiting.

Before he left his village, Snow Boy asked his mother to help him onto a slab of loose ice in the nearby river. Concerned that her son might get hungry, she put a bark container of dry corn next to him. She then gave the chunk of ice a push, sending Snow Boy downstream.

For a long time thereafter, the Lenni-Lenape made annual trips to the river. On each visit, they brought a bark container of corn to offer to Snow Boy. If a slab of ice appeared, they knew Snow Boy had returned. They placed the container of corn on the ice for him to eat. Then they prayed for his help as they tracked game.

would later become famous for writing their history, the Walam Olum, or Red Score, which was a tribal record carved into reeds. To European newcomers, the Lenape were the Indians later known as the Delaware.

The Nanticokes, or tidewater people, roamed land now called Maryland and Delaware. They lived mainly along the Chesapeake Bay in present-day Sussex County. In addition to farming, fishing, and hunting, the Nanticokes were known for bead making. They traded beads of polished shells called wampum to other tribes and later to the Europeans. Wampum was used as money and for belts and jewelry.

The Nanticoke settled near the coast where they farmed, fished, and made wampum, as illustrated here.

NEWCOMERS ARRIVE

In 1609 English navigator Henry Hudson became the first known European to explore the Delaware coast. He had been hired by the Dutch East India Company to find a shorter trade route to East Asia. But his stay in Delaware was brief. The dangerous sandbars of Delaware Bay caused him to veer north where he continued his voyage. The Hudson River in New York is named for this explorer.

A year later, an English sea captain named Samuel Argall from the Virginia Colony sought shelter from a storm in Delaware Bay. Argall named the bay after Virginia's colonial governor, Thomas West, who was third Baron De La Warr. Over the years, the name De La Warr came to be spelled Delaware. The new name referred to the bay and later the large river that flowed into the bay.

Meanwhile, Hudson had sent back news to the Dutch of all his explorations and findings of riches in the new land. Encouraged by these reports, the Dutch sent other expeditions to secure furs for the European market. Traders grew wealthy exchanging iron tools and rum for beaver and other pelts provided by American Indians.

In 1631 a group of twenty-eight Dutch settlers arrived to establish Delaware's first European settlement near the present-day town of Lewes (pronounced LEW-is) on Lewes Creek. Their goal was to make money for the investors who had sponsored their trip and the settlement. The investors hoped the settlers would acquire earnings through trading with Indians and through whaling. The settlers brought cattle, whaling tools, and supplies. The men built a fort and called their settlement Zwaanendael. In their native Dutch that meant "valley of the swans."

On a post outside the fort, the new arrivals placed a metal plaque showing their coat of arms, a very important symbol to Europeans.

Dutch settlers traded goods in exchange for pelts with the American Indians.

The Lenni-Lenape Indians, however, had never before seen such a shiny metal object. One young Lenape was so fascinated by the prize that he brought it back to his village, an act the Dutch considered to be stealing. The Lenni-Lenape man probably thought differently. Historian Carol Hoffecker says, "I think the Indians were just being playful. The Indian saw a tin thing that must have glistened in the sun and he was curious. The Dutch said the Indian who took it should be punished."

The Lenape chief saw the Dutch as allies against their enemies, the warring Susquehannocks. To stay friends with his new neighbors he put to death the man who had taken the coat of arms. The killing angered some Indians so greatly that they attacked all the Dutch settlers, killed their cattle, and burnt their homes and farms, destroying Zwaanendael.

NEW SWEDEN

In 1638 two Swedish ships arrived in the region. The Swedes came with the same intent as had the Dutch: to settle and earn money. But these settlers developed a more peaceful relationship with the American Indians. They brought muskets and other trade goods to promote hunting by the natives. This in turn gave the Swedes a source of valuable pelts. At the same time, the Swedes settled along a river that they named after their ruler, Queen Christina. They chopped down trees to construct strong log houses and built Fort Christina on a site that is now Wilmington. Homes in this settlement are believed to have been the first log cabins in the New World.

As the Swedes gained a foothold in the region, the Dutch continued to settle more land. In 1651 they built Fort Casimir near Fort Christina, close to present-day New Castle. This began a fierce rivalry between Dutch and Swedish settlers. The Swedes eventually captured Fort Casimir. But a year later, the Dutch recaptured it and continued battling until they took control

Swedish ships Kalmar Nyckel *and* Fogel Grip *arrived at the mouth of the Delaware River in 1638.*

of Fort Christina. They built the small town of Amstel nearby. The Swedes never again held power in the area.

While the Swedes and Dutch were fighting over this territory, England watched closely. By the mid-1600s, the English controlled most of the colonies on the eastern seaboard and regarded the Dutch as intruders. Delaware was one slice of land they were missing. With its access to water, Delaware was very appealing for trade.

In 1664 the English sailed down from New Amsterdam (present-day New York), and captured New Amstel. Then in 1682 England's King Charles II granted William Penn a large chunk of land for purposes of colonization. The territory, which lay to the north and west of the Delaware River, was originally named Penn's Silvania, which means "Penn's Woods." Soon it became Pennsylvania.

Penn's colonists survey their newly granted land.

PENN IS MIGHTIER THAN THE SWORD

Penn belonged to a sect called the Religious Society of Friends, or Quakers. Quakers are pacifists, meaning that they rejected all forms of violence, especially war. Penn had hopes that Pennsylvania would be a place where people of all religions and backgrounds would get along in friendship. He made a strong effort to stay on good terms with the American Indians. He once wrote to members of the Lenni-Lenape, "I desire to gain your love and friendship by a kind, just and peaceable life."

Yet Penn had one problem with his newly acquired land of brotherhood: Pennsylvania did not have a river that led to the ocean. The British Crown gave the Quaker leader control of Delaware land, too. Penn split his new land into three counties: New Castle, Kent, and Sussex. They became known as the Three Lower Counties of Pennsylvania.

Most people in the Three Lower Counties made their living by farming. They grew wheat, rye, and corn. They also raised beef and harvested lumber. Some, mainly in southern Delaware, owned African slaves who did the backbreaking labor.

According to legend, Penn met with Chief Tamenend in 1682 to sign a treaty of friendship with the Delaware. Under the arrangement, Penn paid the chief for the American-Indian land the English king gave him in exchange for wampum belts. This treaty did not stop Europeans from wanting additional Lenni-Lenape land. As more Europeans came, other treaties were made and broken. Europeans grabbed Delaware territory and pushed the Lenni-Lenape from their homeland.

DELAWARE AND THE AMERICAN REVOLUTION

Towns in the Delaware region thrived. But no town in the Three Lower Counties prospered as much as Philadelphia, the biggest city in the

Pennsylvania Colony. Feeling powerless in comparison to the mighty businesses and government based in Philadelphia, residents of the Three Lower Counties complained to William Penn. He decided to allow the three counties some independence. They would remain part of Pennsylvania but could have more control over policies that affected their towns. Thereafter, Delaware had its own assembly but shared a governor with Pennsylvania. Penn rarely visited Delaware and did not exercise much authority there.

Similar requests for independence erupted across the American colonies. For a long time, the British Crown had let the colonists more or less govern themselves. However, in the early 1760s England became

Penn meets with colonists of the Three Lower Counties as they voice their concerns regarding independence.

involved in a costly war with France. England needed money to pay soldiers and to manufacture weapons to fight the war. King George III imposed heavy taxes on the colonies to raise money. Since the colonists had no voice in British government, they protested this "taxation without representation."

Tensions between the colonists and England boiled over. Colonists seriously debated cutting all ties to the Crown. On July 2, 1776, delegates from all the colonies were scheduled to vote in Philadelphia over whether to declare independence. One of Delaware's three delegates to the Continental Congress, Caesar Rodney, made a legendary ride to Philadelphia to vote on this historic matter. Independence was declared, and George Washington took charge of the new Continental Army. One month later, on August 23, King George III declared the colonies traitors and sent soldiers to put down the revolt. Representatives from the Three Lower Counties demanded more than the other colonies that same year. They voted to separate from Pennsylvania as well as from England. They became a separate colony named Delaware.

Colonists celebrate the Declaration of Independence in Dover.

THE BLUE HENS OF DELAWARE

Delaware's state bird is the blue hen chicken. According to legend, this bird's history goes back to the American Revolution and Delaware soldiers who fought against the British. Only one battle took place in Delaware during the Revolution. Still, the colony's men gained a reputation as some of the war's fiercest soldiers, legendary for their bravery.

Captain Jonathon Caldwell's company amused themselves when not fighting by holding cockfights with blue-feathered chickens. In cockfighting, people bet on which of two roosters (or gamecocks) will fight the other to the death. Today, cock-fighting is regarded as cruel and is outlawed in many places. In the 1700s, this was not the case.

During the cockfights, soldiers noticed that blue hens proved to be fearless fighters. Gamecocks whose mothers were blue hens were said to be the strongest of any fighting birds. Delaware's soldiers compared themselves to the tough, disciplined roosters. The birds attacked each other much as the military company battled the British. So the Continental Regiment of Delaware called themselves the "blue hens' chickens," cementing the name in history. In 1939 Delaware lawmakers made the blue-feathered creature the state bird to recognize the state's role in the Revolutionary War and creating the nation.

During the American Revolution very little fighting took place in Delaware. The only encounter of note was the Battle of Cooch's Bridge, which was fought on September 3, 1777, outside Newark. The British won that battle and soon seized the city of Wilmington as well. Within weeks, England's naval fleet was anchored off northern Delaware. Because the British fleet was so near, the Delaware legislature moved from New Castle in the north to Dover in the central part of the colony. Dover remains Delaware's capital to this day.

AFTER THE WAR

The American Revolution ended in 1783, and the colonies won their independence. Now they needed a way to govern themselves. In 1787 delegates from the thirteen colonies held a convention to draft the U.S. Constitution. Delaware was the first colony to ratify (or approve) the Constitution. Because of its quick action in accepting the nation's founding document, Delaware is known as the First State.

In the infant years of the new country, the people of Delaware tended to their lives and jobs. As in most places then, the way Delaware residents made money depended on geography. The three main elements of Delaware's geography were the ocean, the trees, and the rushing waterways in the north.

The nearness to large bodies of water resulted in Delawareans developing a shipbuilding industry during the late 1700s and early 1800s. In the north, mills continued to turn wheat into flour. In 1785 a creative Delawarean named Oliver Evans invented more efficient automatic milling machinery. His inventions helped make flour even faster.

Another enterprising young man came to Delaware in 1800. His name was Éleuthère Irénée du Pont. Du Pont was from a wealthy family in France.

THE BOMBING OF LEWES—1813

During the War of 1812, the British navy attempted to blockade the entire American coast. Lewes, situated at the mouth of Delaware Bay, occupied a strategic position, blocking access to Dover, Wilmington, and farther upstream, Philadelphia. On a blustery day in March 1813, the captain of a British frigate anchored in Lewes harbor and demanded that the townspeople furnish supplies for his ship and crew. He was astounded when they refused. A song told how brave—and stubborn—Delawareans were.

Words by Gilbert Byron　　　　　　　　　　　　**Music by Jerry Silverman**

During the war of eigh-teen twelve, A Brit-ish fleet sailed in the bay,

Trained its guns on old Lew-es town, Gave the peo-ple just one day To

furn-ish twen-ty bull-ocks, fat, Man-y hogs-heads of wa-ter, sweet.

Eith-er yield to the king's re-quest, Or to the guns of the

Colonel Samuel Davis answered, "No!"
He'd never feed a British mouth,
And trained his little twelve pounders
Toward the big fleet in the south.
With that the British fleet opened up,
Two hundred and forty cannon boomed,
Solid lead screamed overhead,
Fire rockets whistled, shrapnel boomed.

But their aim was so atrocious,
After twenty-two hours of this squeeze,
A hound dog and a setting hen
Were the only casualties.
While the citizens picked solid ball
From the streets like manna bread,
And the little guns of Lewes
Gave the British back their lead.

And when the British marines tried to land,
The citizens turned them back.
Old men paraded with cornstalks,
British eyes were fooled by that.
They raised their sails so silently,
Slipped out of the Delaware Bay,
And they never came back again—
At least not in our day.

And just to add my little iron,
The British commander's name was Byron.

His father, Pierre-Samuel du Pont de Nemours, had emigrated from France and had become friends with such national founders as Benjamin Franklin and Thomas Jefferson.

The younger du Pont built a gunpowder mill on Brandywine Creek near Wilmington. In time he constructed more powder mills. Several du Ponts died in explosions, for this was a dangerous way to make money. Yet when the United States began fighting England in the War of 1812, Du Pont powder mills served the young nation well and put a bang into Delaware's economy.

In 1802 the Du Pont Company established their first gunpowder mills on the Brandywine Creek.

THE CREATED RIVER

A visitor to northern Delaware in the early 1800s would have been struck by the many sawmills, paper mills, cotton mills, powder mills, and flour mills. Wilmington also became known for its leather goods and its fine carriages. Moving all these products to places where they were needed, however, was a great concern. There were no trucks or trains then. But there were steamships. The steamship in the early 1800s was built with state-of-the-art technology.

Steamships sailing between Wilmington and Philadelphia followed an easy route along the Delaware River. But ships traveling from Wilmington to Washington, D.C., or Baltimore had a long trip. They journeyed south on the Delaware River into Delaware Bay and the Atlantic Ocean. Then they sailed around the Delmarva Peninsula before heading north through the Chesapeake Bay to the two cities.

Steamships were used as a means to transport people and goods from Delaware to Philadelphia and Washington, D.C.

To ease travel, the state needed another waterway like the Delaware River. Lawmakers suggested a channel to connect the Chesapeake Bay and Delaware River. From 1824 to 1829 teams of workers dug an artificial river, or canal, across the northern neck of the Delmarva Peninsula. The channel was called the Chesapeake and Delaware Canal (later known as the C & D Canal). This canal still separates northern and southern Delaware.

SLAVERY AND FREEDOM

Like many states before 1865, Delaware permitted slavery. In states of the Deep South, African slaves worked plantations. The region's economy depended on unpaid slave labor. But Delaware was a border state, located partly in the antislavery North and partly in the South. While some farmers in southern Delaware used slave labor, most Delawareans were against slavery. The state constitution of 1776 read, "No person hereafter imported into this state from Africa ought to be held in slavery . . . and no . . . slave ought to be brought into this state from any part of the world." Yet, many Delawareans ignored this caution.

Slaves in Delaware often experienced freedoms and privileges unavailable farther south. Many people taught their slaves a trade or how to read. The black population found strong support from many state leaders who wished to abolish slavery entirely. As a result of this antislavery climate, the number of slaves in Delaware dropped from 9,000 in 1790 to 1,798 in 1860. But votes always fell short of ending the practice in Delaware. Some whites worried that they could one day be outnumbered, hence outvoted should the slaves be freed and allowed to vote.

TWO DELAWAREANS: DIFFERENT PATHS

The different viewpoints regarding slavery in the First State are represented by two famous Delawareans. One was a woman named Lucretia "Patty" Cannon. For decades, she and a band of outlaws kidnapped free black men, women, and children and sold them into slavery. She was captured but died in prison awaiting trial.

Thomas Garrett followed a different path. He was a devout Quaker who helped more than two thousand slaves escape by way of the Underground Railroad. The Underground Railroad was not a train. Instead, it was a network of places, or stations, where slaves were sheltered while fleeing from their owners to freedom in the North and Canada. Garrett's home in Wilmington was among the last of these havens before travelers reached Pennsylvania, where slavery was outlawed.

Since slaves were considered property in Delaware, Garrett was breaking the law by helping them escape from their owners. He was found guilty of theft in 1848 and ordered to pay a heavy fine. Garrett lost nearly everything he owned, but he had no regrets. He said he would continue to help any slaves he could. And he did.

THE CIVIL WAR AND ITS AFTERMATH

The issue of slavery came to a head when Abraham Lincoln, a Republican, was elected president in November 1860. Lincoln ran on a strong antislavery platform. Fearing that they would lose the right to own slaves, several Southern states left the United States to form their own country, which they called the Confederate States of America. In April 1861, the Confederates attacked Fort Sumter in South Carolina. This attack began the Civil War.

Although Delaware was a slave state, it stayed in the Union. Historian Carol Hoffecker says, "Delaware was mainly pro-Union, but some in southern Delaware were pro-Confederacy. Others disagreed with Lincoln's policy of one nation that should end slavery. They felt that if the South wanted to leave, they should be allowed to."

Once again, as in the Revolutionary War, Delaware experienced no major battles on state soil. One of Delaware's greatest contributions to the war effort was gunpowder made at the Du Pont mills.

The Du Pont Company made great contributions to the Civil War by providing gunpowder to the Union army.

The Du Pont Company supplied an estimated one-third to one-half of all gunpowder used by the North.

After the war, Delaware proved to be more like the Old South than the industrial North in its attitude toward black people. For example, the Delaware legislature passed a poll tax that people had to pay to be able to vote. Many African Americans could not afford to pay the tax. Those who could pay were often ignored by tax collectors. At the same time, many whites were not asked to pay the tax.

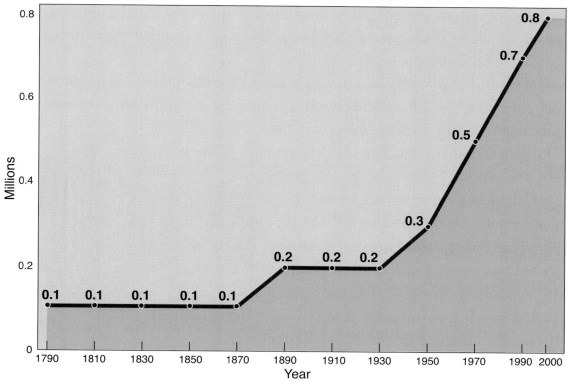

POPULATION GROWTH: 1790–2000

A GAME OF MONOPOLY

Over the next several decades, northern Delaware became a hotbed of industrial growth. Factories in and around Wilmington made steel, railroad cars, ships, and paper. And the Du Pont powder works continued to thrive. The company became so successful that it had virtually no competition. That kind of situation is called a monopoly.

In 1907 the federal government sued the Du Pont Company gunpowder business under the Sherman Anti-Trust Act, which banned monopolies. The law reinforced the idea that competition among providers improves products and services for everyone. Du Pont, the government successfully claimed, was a monopoly under the terms of the law. Du Pont lost the lawsuit. To continue operating, the company split into the Hercules and Atlas powder-making businesses. In addition, Du Pont expanded into another profitable business: chemicals.

The du Ponts' chemical business was very successful, like the gunpowder enterprise. By the early twentieth century, the du Ponts were the most prominent family in Delaware, and the Du Pont Company was famous throughout the world. (Although the du Ponts spell their last name with a lowercase d, the company name uses a capital D.) Perhaps Du Pont's greatest chemical invention was nylon, created in a Seaford plant in 1938. During World War II, nylon was key in making parachutes, flak jackets, tires, and other war products. Today nylon is used in pantyhose and many other consumer and industrial goods.

After the Civil War, Delaware became an industrial power. Here shipbuilders construct a steamship in Wilmington.

DELAWARE'S FIRST FAMILY

At the same time the Du Pont organization expanded its reach, members of the du Pont family were becoming community leaders and active in state politics. Several du Ponts gave money to Delaware's institutions and joined their boards. Three cousins, all great-grandsons of Éleuthère (below), donated fortunes to bettering the state. T. Coleman du Pont used his money to build a major two-lane highway from Wilmington to the Maryland border. He donated the highway to the government for public use. When a state pension program broke down Alfred I. du Pont gave his money to the elderly and disabled children. Later, his estate became the Du Pont Hospital for Children. Pierre Samuel du Pont donated large sums of money to Delaware's school system.

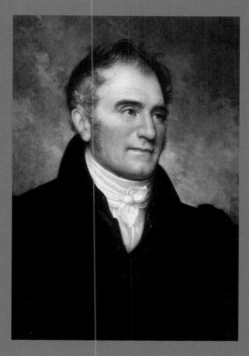

Today, the du Pont family shows no signs of losing its financial power, although the company is run by others. Every so often, magazines publish the names of the five hundred wealthiest people in the United States. Usually, ten to twelve members of the du Pont family make the list.

RACE RELATIONS INTO THE TWENTY-FIRST CENTURY

After World War II ended in 1945, race relations became a major issue across the United States. African Americans had had enough of living under segregation (separation of the races). Though Delaware separated blacks and whites less openly than in many regions of the country, there were areas of concern. In the early postwar era, laws required separation of races in the state's public schools, theaters, and restaurants. In 1963 a Delaware court ruled that segregation in public places, including schools, was against the law.

Laws and court decisions did not always change people's attitudes. School segregation, especially in two southern counties, was not completely ended until the mid-1960s. In the mid- and late 1960s, "white flight" infected Wilmington. A large number of whites, unwilling to live among African Americans in urban neighborhoods, moved to the suburbs.

At the same time, blacks in Wilmington and other cities were limited to lower-paying jobs because they lacked the opportunities open to whites. Blacks wanted the same chances as whites to improve their lifestyles, but the future looked bleak. Blacks grew

Prior to 1963 Delaware's schools were segregated as can be seen from this photo taken in 1949 at Pierre S. Dupont High School in Wilmington.

more and more frustrated and angry, inner cities across America erupted in violence. A Delaware civil rights activist named Roger Wilkins said, "Generations of heaping inferiority into our souls needed to be purged. And if you're going to put that awful stuff into people, when people begin to expel it, it's not coming out pretty."

Riots hit Wilmington in April 1968 after the murder of civil rights leader Martin Luther King Jr. As a result, Delaware was forced to make changes. State lawmakers passed a fair-housing law that made it illegal to deny a person a home solely because of race. One of the boldest policies was called urban homesteading. Cities awarded people houses that were in poor shape free of charge. The only condition was that they spend money to make the dwelling livable. Observers say the program had mixed success.

ECONOMIC PROGESS

Over the next few decades, tourism and banking joined chemicals and manufacturing as the state's biggest industries. A few other businesses made their mark in Delaware, too. In 1997 Delaware entered into an arrangement with Pennsylvania to develop more ports along the Delaware River. Both states hoped to increase traffic from international shipping lines, leading to new jobs for their residents and funds coming into the states.

More recently, a few new companies have been drawn to the Delaware River region. They contrast with chemical plants of the early twentieth century that still operate. One major addition has been the storage products manufacturer Zenith Products. According to the *New York Times*, the company's Briggs Pletcher reported that "Zenith was attracted to the riverfront for reasons of highway access and esthetics."

With increased population and industry came road construction and housing developments. Four-lane highways and buildings covered farmland.

The old and the new share a place along the Christina River in Wilmington.

Some complained that growth was ruining Delaware. Author Eric Zencey interviewed Nicolas DiPasquale, former head of the state department of natural resources, in 2002. DiPasquale believed that suburban sprawl harmed the state environment more than the chemical industry. He said, "Vinyl [is] popping up all over the place."

On the positive side, Delaware is joining the rest of the country in offering what other states have. In 2000 Delaware elected its first woman governor, Ruth Ann Minner, and reelected her four years later. Only a handful of states can make that claim. In 2002 state lawmakers passed a smoking ban in public places, further bringing Delaware into the modern—and healthier—age. Today, diversity in terms of both race and the economy enriches Delaware's character.

Chapter Three
People of Delaware

Many think people from given states or regions have certain recognizable traits. But whereas Texans have a cowboy image and Coloradans their outdoor spirit, no common stereotype of Delawareans comes to mind. Delaware has always been a fairly diverse state in terms of religious and immigrant groups. Of course, no single characteristic fits everyone in a given state, inside or out of Delaware. The real story is much more interesting.

NORTH AND SOUTH

According to 2006 U.S. government figures, 853,476 people live in Delaware. The state ranks forty-fifth of the fifty states in population. However, Delaware holds a small but steady population growth rate.

In terms of character, the people of Delaware appear to be divided into two sets. Even Delaware residents often refer to people from their home state as being from "above the canal" or "below the canal," referring to the Chesapeake and Delaware Canal.

The Delaware State Fair is a great place to celebrate all that is Delaware.

Whether from above or below the canal, all Delawareans take pride in their state.

Journalist Norman Lockman says, "As far as the north versus south mentality, Delaware is a kind of unique microcosm [little world] of the country. People above the canal tend to behave like people from Connecticut. People from the bottom part of the state tend to behave more like people from Georgia."

Above the canal are the cities of Wilmington and Newark, with their wealthy suburbs and miles of industrial facilities. Delaware above the canal involves a smaller portion of the state, but it is home to most of the state's population. Below the canal, the only city of any significant size is Dover, the capital, whose estimated population in 2006 was 34,735.

The rest of Delaware below the canal contains small towns, tidy villages, and beach resorts. The overwhelming majority of the land is devoted to agriculture, unlike the more industrial north. The people living to the south tend to have a different attitude about life and politics. Lockman notes, "The bottom part of the state is conservative [traditional]. The top part of the state, while not liberal by any standards, is more moderate."

Southern Delaware is an agricultural region, unlike the industrial north.

ETHNIC DELAWARE

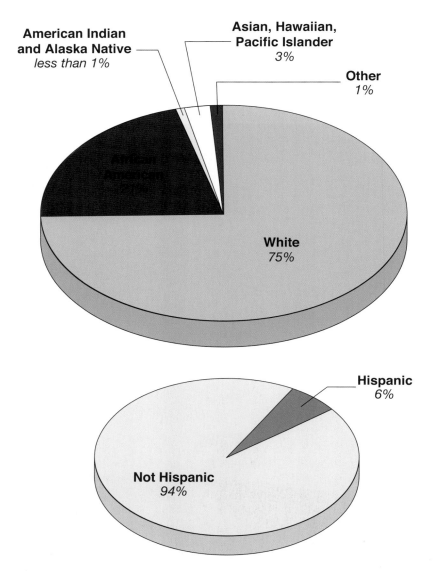

American Indian
and Alaska Native
less than 1%

Asian, Hawaiian,
Pacific Islander
3%

Other
1%

African
American
21%

White
75%

Hispanic
6%

Not Hispanic
94%

*Note: A person of Cuban, Mexican, Puerto Rican, South or Central American,
or other Spanish culture or origin, regardless of race, is defined as Hispanic.*

EARLY SETTLERS TO RECENT IMMIGRANTS

The population of Delaware has changed greatly since the Swedes, Dutch, and English battled over the land three centuries ago. Still, many residents speak of these and other ancestors who traveled to the state in the days before independence.

The first sizable wave of immigration in the 1700s brought Scotch-Irish settlers. In addition, blacks, some free and some enslaved, totaled about 20 percent of the population by 1790. As Wilmington became an important port, more people emigrated from different countries. Over the next 150 years, scores of newcomers arrived from Ireland, Germany, Poland, Russia, and Italy. In the last several decades, there has been an influx of Hispanics, mostly from Puerto Rico and Guatemala, and Asians.

A Puerto Rican family celebrates their culture and heritage at a parade in Wilmington.

ANNIE JUMP CANNON: FAMOUS STARGAZER

Dover-born Annie Jump Cannon gained attention in 1880 when, at age sixteen, she became one of the first women from Delaware to attend college. She graduated from Wellesley College in Massachusetts, a huge achievement for a woman back then. But she went on to gain acclaim as a skilled scientist.

Cannon held a job at the Harvard College Observatory in Cambridge, Massachusetts. She gained a reputation for working at record speed. Between 1911 and 1915, she classified an average of five thousand stars a month. Scientists believe that Cannon, who was known as the Census Taker of the Sky, cataloged about 350,000 stars during her lifetime. She developed a system of cataloging stars that is still used today. Astronomers credit her with being the first astronomer to prove that most stars can be classified by color.

Of the many honors Cannon acquired, she treasured being the first woman to receive an honorary doctorate from the highly respected Oxford University in England. She understood that her place as a woman in history as a scientist was important and always encouraged those who came after her. In 1932 Cannon donated prize money she had won to the American Astronomical Society to fund a prize for women in astronomy.

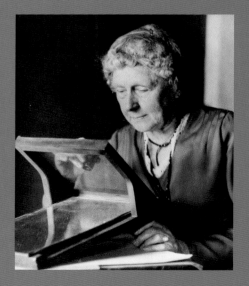

Cannon died in 1941 when World War II raged in Europe. Perhaps that is why she said just before her death, "In our troubled days it is good to have something outside our planet, something fine and distant for comfort."

Today, about three of every four Delaware residents are white, as are the vast majority of the residents from rural Kent and Sussex counties. In 2006, 21 percent of the population was African American, 6.3 percent Hispanic or Latino, 2.8 percent Asian, and 1.4 percent from mixed-race homes.

Most African Americans live in the Wilmington area. Of 72,664 total Wilmington residents, 41,001 are black. The black population of Wilmington in New Castle County is roughly equal to the African-American population of Kent and Sussex counties combined.

LIVING TOGETHER

Delaware has taken several steps to improve race relations. The YWCA of New Castle County sponsored serious discussions in a format called race study circles "to promote respectful dialogue and problem solve" ways to help people get along better. The discussion groups provided an open, respectful environment where participants could try to understand other people's cultures and points of view.

Small breakthroughs have occurred since then. In 1992 Jim Sills became the first African-American mayor of Wilmington. He was reelected in 1996. After his term, Wilmington residents elected two more African-American mayors and two city council presidents.

In a similar spirit of embracing differences, the city of Dover declared September 19, 2000 Race Equality Day. The stated goal was "to urge citizens to join together to reaffirm a commitment to ensuring racial equality and justice." By 2004 there had been additional signs of improvement. Delaware awarded Gregory Chambers a social issue award for expanding study circles to other state agencies, including the Delaware state police. Most participants believe that the circles have increased their understanding of others' beliefs and attitudes.

PEACH CRISP

Thanks to many years as a peach-growing center, peach recipes are popular in Delaware. Ask an adult to help prepare this tasty treat.

    5 peaches cut into slices
    2 tablespoons flour
    1/3 cup brown sugar
    2/3 cup gingersnap or vanilla wafer crumbs
    1/2 cup uncooked oatmeal
    1 teaspoon ground cinnamon
    3 tablespoons softened butter

Preheat oven to 350 °F. Toss peach slices with flour and place in a 9 inch x 9 inch pan. Combine oatmeal, brown sugar, gingersnaps, and cinnamon in a bowl. Cut butter into the mixture until it looks like large crumbs. Spread the oat mixture over the peaches. Bake about 25 minutes or until the topping is light brown.

People of all races have entered the program believing themselves to be without racial biases. But they have come away thinking about their everyday activities and responses to situations differently. Lynn Paul, who has taken part in several circles, says, "It's probably the first time in your life you can put yourself in someone else's shoes. It gives you an opportunity to listen and say, 'Oh, so that's why you feel that way.'"

AMISH AND AMERICAN INDIANS

Most Amish people live in Pennsylvania and Ohio, but about two hundred Amish families farm in the countryside west of Dover. Amish are strict Protestants who take every word of the Bible literally. Unlike most Americans, the Amish deny themselves modern conveniences and pleasures.

The Amish in Delaware lead a life without modern conveniences, such as television and computers.

POPULATION DENSITY

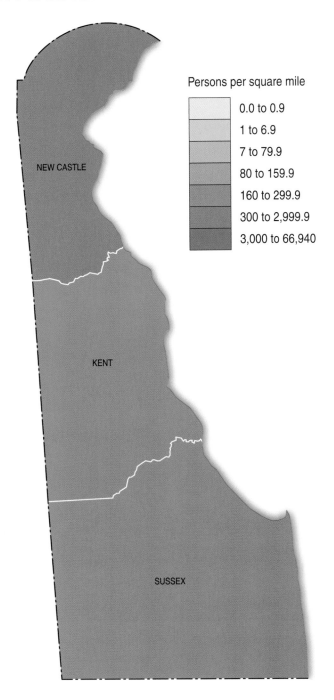

Persons per square mile

	0.0 to 0.9
	1 to 6.9
	7 to 79.9
	80 to 159.9
	160 to 299.9
	300 to 2,999.9
	3,000 to 66,940

NEW CASTLE

KENT

SUSSEX

They live without televisions, computers, radios, washing machines, and cars. They travel by foot or by horse and buggy. They run their homes and businesses without electricity. Moreover, they believe strongly in nonviolence. Because of this, they do not serve in the military.

Most Amish men work as farmers and builders. Amish children attend school, usually one-room schoolhouses, only until the eighth grade. Amish people of all ages reject clothes that are brightly colored and short skirts and trousers. Even in the heat of summer, they cover up in long-sleeved dark clothing from head to toe.

Sometimes, travelers can see Amish people driving along the two-lane roads of central Delaware in their buggies. On Tuesdays and Fridays of most weeks, Amish homemade foods, such as sausages, baked goods, and preserves, are sold at an open-air market in Dover.

Amish people farm and travel with machinery from settler days.

CANNOLI, PIZZA, AND MUSIC

One of Delaware's biggest ethnic festivals takes place every June in Wilmington. The event is called Saint Anthony's Festa Italiana, and the setting is the grounds of Saint Anthony of Padua Roman Catholic Church.

In addition to carnival rides, the festival hosts a parade and six outdoor cafés, each one serving a different type of Italian food. Visitors munch on everything from pizza and chicken spezzato to pastries, such as cannoli. Live bands perform a different type of Italian music at each café. At one café customers hear opera. Other cafés may feature popular modern Italian songs.

The festival began in 1933 and was simply Il Carnevale. Over the next few decades the celebration expanded to include various restaurants, musical entertainment, and Italian products, including ceramics from Salerno, Italy, Wilmington's sister city. The carnival has since grown into a huge event, with more than 300,000 visitors attending over eight days. Money from the carnival has funded many church and school projects.

By the 1990s the festival was named a "Top 50" attraction in North America by the American Bus Tour Association. Today it is one of the highlights of the Brandywine Valley. Many visitors are former Wilmington residents who return every year for this special event.

Like every other state, Delaware retains a population of those who were here first, American Indians. Today, most Delaware Indians live among the Cherokee in Oklahoma. But southwestern Delaware contains a tribe of roughly five hundred Nanticoke Indians. The Nanticoke are best known to other Delawareans for the annual powwows held in September. At the powwow, the American Indians from many eastern tribes demonstrate their crafts, foods, and customs to visitors of all backgrounds. Storytelling and ceremonial dancing are popular activities at the event.

A Nanticoke performs a traditional dance at a powwow in Riverdale.

Chapter Four

Inside Government

Delaware's government was built on the state motto, "Liberty and Independence." In 1787 Delaware became the first state to ratify or vote to approve the Constitution of the United States. Therefore, it's no surprise that the state government adopted in 1792 worked in much the same way as the U.S. government. Several changes have occurred since then, but much of the current constitution dates back to 1897. Today, Delaware government is divided into three branches: executive, legislative, and judicial.

EXECUTIVE BRANCH

The chief executive of Delaware is the governor, who is elected by voters for a four-year team. The governor can serve no more than two terms.

The governor's main job is to either sign or reject bills passed by the legislative branch of government. A bill that the governor vetoes, or rejects, can still pass, however, if three-fifths of each body in the legislative branch votes to override the veto. Another key job of the governor is to appoint state judges, heads of departments, and other officials who carry out the business of state government.

Legislative Hall in Dover is the seat of Delaware's government.

Ruth Ann Minner has been Delaware's governor since 2001. A main goal of her office has been to improve and extend education. In 2005 she signed a law that gave students who stay out of trouble and keep good grades a free college education. She also authorized state schools to provide full-day kindergarten, a breakthrough for working parents and for students whose families cannot afford preschool.

Governor Ruth Ann Minner speaks to the General Assembly in Legislative Hall in January 2006.

A TRUE DELAWARE CUSTOM

Because Delaware is small, it can maintain traditions that would be unworkable in larger states. A perfect example is Return Day, which takes place two days after every general election. The beginnings of Return Day date to the days before computers, television, or even radio. Back then, citizens had to travel to their county seats to hear election results.

Today, upward of ten thousand Delaware citizens show up for the festivities in the Sussex County community of Georgetown. In a show of goodwill, both winning and losing candidates ride together through the center of town in a parade of horse-drawn carriages and floats. Following the parade, speeches are given and final vote totals are formally announced. Everyone then shares in a bull roast.

In the evening, parties take place throughout Georgetown. Republicans and Democrats dance and socialize with each other in the spirit of friendship and cooperation. Even Delaware's U.S. senators, congressional representative, and governor usually show up for Return Day even if they didn't have to run in the election. The day stands as a tribute to democracy and the peaceful exchange of power that occurs in the United States.

LEGISLATIVE BRANCH

The state legislature is called the Delaware General Assembly. The assembly is divided into two bodies: a senate and a house of representatives. Voters select both bodies. The forty-one representatives serve two-year terms, while the twenty-one senators serve four-year terms.

The Senate and the House of Representatives make up Delaware's General Assembly. They meet in Legislative Hall in Dover.

The chief job of the Delaware General Assembly is to pass and reject laws. The assembly also supervises departments created to support and carry out the daily functions of this body. For example, the controller's office handles matters relating to money and budgets. Researchers provide information to both houses of the assembly to help lawmakers make decisions.

JUDICIAL BRANCH

Like the federal government, Delaware has a supreme court as its highest court. Delaware's Supreme Court has five justices who serve twelve-year terms. All judges are nominated by the governor and confirmed by the Delaware General Assembly. To ensure a balance of Democrats and Republicans in the highest court, three of the justices must represent one party, while the other two justices must be members of the other one.

DELAWARE BY COUNTY

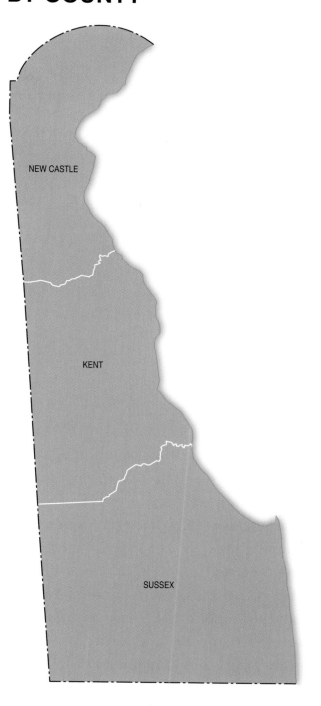

NEW CASTLE

KENT

SUSSEX

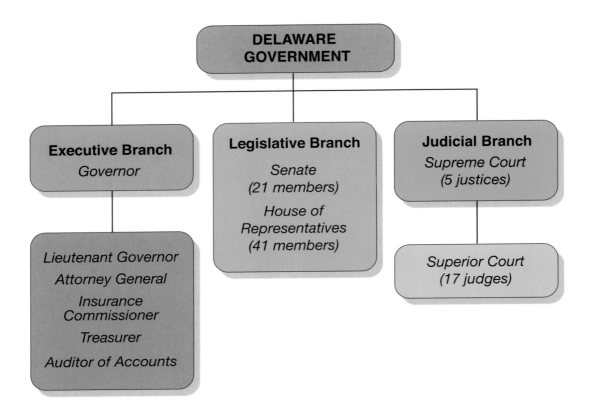

The job of the supreme court justices is to hear appeals to decisions made in Delaware's lower courts.

There are several lower state courts in Delaware. The supreme court, the next below the supreme court, hears all major cases involving criminal activity, personal injury, and libel. The superior court also hears appeals from lower courts across the state.

The court of chancery makes decisions in matters relating to land sales, estates, and business disputes. The court of common pleas hears cases involving minor offenses or disputes between people. Cases regarding family relations are heard in family court.

THE SAMANTHA CASE

A Delaware Family Court case made national news in the late 1990s. A ten-year-old girl named Samantha had been abandoned at age six by her mother, who was a drug addict. For the next four years Samantha lived in four foster homes, including one in which she may have been abused. Samantha saw a counselor, who helped her cope with the problems in her life. In time the counselor grew to love Samantha and wanted to adopt her.

Samantha sued to "divorce" her mother so she could live with her counselor. However, by the time Samantha reached age ten, her mother was recovering from her addiction and wanted custody of Samantha. The Delaware Family Court decided that Samantha should be united with her mother.

Samantha appealed to the state supreme court, and national children's rights groups took her side and helped her make a case. On June 19, 1998, the state's highest court ruled in Samantha's favor.

Within a few weeks, however, Samantha and her mother reconciled. Samantha agreed to move in with her mother, who lives in another state. Around the same time, Delaware governor Thomas Carper signed a law making it easier for children abandoned by their parents to divorce them. The new law forces the family court to consider whether a child would be emotionally harmed if forced to live with neglectful parents.

Chapter Five

Conducting Business in Delaware

Delaware is a good state in which to reside and earn a living. Delawareans rank fourteenth in the nation, with an average yearly income of slightly more than $50,000. The state's ability to remain prosperous even in rough economic times comes from the state's diverse economy.

Manufacturing, once a major growth area, now shares prominence with finance, insurance, and real estate businesses. Agriculture and fishing still contribute large amounts to Delaware's product line. The Dover Air Force Base remains one of the state's major employers. As a reflection of its healthy economy, Delaware is one of the few states that has no sales tax. "I loved that when I went to college in Delaware. It was the home of tax-free shopping," remembers Ralph von dem Hagen, now a Pennsylvania resident.

A BOOMING ECONOMY

Wilmington has always been the heart of the state's economy. Du Pont headquartered its business there in the early nineteenth century.

Some agriculture supports a percentage of Delaware's economy.

2006 GROSS STATE PRODUCT: $60 Million

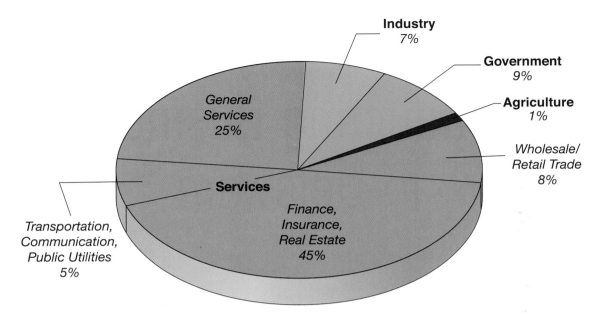

Industry 7%

Government 9%

Agriculture 1%

Wholesale/ Retail Trade 8%

General Services 25%

Services

Finance, Insurance, Real Estate 45%

Transportation, Communication, Public Utilities 5%

Other manufacturers of food, rubber, plastics, paper, and metal products opened plants in the area. So the state sometimes has taken a special interest in keeping the city vital and healthy.

An example of urban renewal was the First USA Riverfront Arts Center. The center was another of several developments along the Brandywine and Christina rivers in Wilmington that were designed to attract tourists and revitalize the city's decaying waterfront. The Brandywine Christina Gateway project appeared at either end of Market Street beginning in the late 1970s. The First USA Riverfront Arts Center opened in 1998 with 87,000 square feet of galleries, gift shops, restaurants, and meeting and convention rooms.

As a sign of what the center could bring to Wilmington residents, its first major traveling exhibit displayed treasures that had belonged to

LOCATION MEANS EVERYTHING

Wilmington, the state's biggest city and major banking center, has something else in its favor when it comes to conducting business: location. Journalist Norman Lockman says, "Wilmington is a very easy city to get in and out of. There is a joke that goes that Wilmington is an easy place to do business in because you can leave it so easily."

Wilmington is roughly midway between New York City and Washington, D.C. At most, it's a forty-minute drive from Philadelphia International Airport. Route I-95, the main north-south interstate highway along the East Coast, runs through downtown.

Wilmington is also one of the few American cities to rely heavily on passenger rail service. Amtrak's Metroliner, a high-speed train that can travel up to 125 miles per hour, stops at Wilmington fifteen times a day on runs to and from New York City and Washington. Travelers can leave New York on the Metroliner and be in Wilmington in about an hour and a half. "It's very handy for people who have to do commerce here," says Lockman.

the Romanovs, the last royal family of Russia who were forced from power in 1918. On view were items such as the Russian imperial throne and a two-hundred-year-old gilded coach. Before the arts center was built, this type of exhibition would have bypassed Wilmington for a big city, such as New York or Washington, D.C. Other major exhibits followed. Now the arts center attracts people from all over the Northeast and Mid-Atlantic states.

In an effort to boost Wilmington's economy, the city added Christina Crossing Retail Center in 2007. This most recent of several developments boasts a 70,000-square-foot grocery store with an additional 50,000 square feet of retail space. This project is designed to enliven the neighborhood in an effort to draw more residents. Similar projects are popping up throughout Delaware as more people think about living and working in the First State.

DELAWARE WORKFORCE

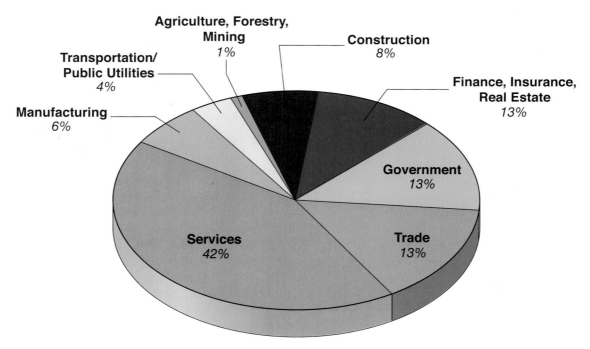

AT WORK IN DELAWARE

For decades, most people assumed that anyone with a job in Delaware worked for Du Pont. To outsiders, the du Ponts seemed to own the state of Delaware. Deborah Haskell of the state heritage commission admits that "for a long time that impression was somewhat accurate." Delaware was basically a company town. Wilmington is sometimes called the chemical capital of the world.

Now things have changed—for Du Pont and for Delaware. Like many major corporations, Du Pont has gone from doing business in one state to having plants and offices worldwide. In addition, Du Pont, like many American businesses, laid off many workers in the early 1990s. Some scientists who lost jobs at Du Pont started their own chemical research businesses.

An employee at Du Pont spools threads of Lyrca.

Today, many people who don't remember Du Pont's dominance in Delaware associate the First State with different kinds of business: banking, finance, and insurance. Financial services account for about 41 percent of the state's economy. Two major changes motivated growth in this area.

Delaware's emergence as a banking center began in 1981 when Governor Pierre S. "Pete" du Pont signed the Financial Center Development Act (FCDA). The FCDA revolutionized the banking industry. Most states had limits on the interest rates banks could charge customers. The FCDA removed all limits for banks located in Delaware. Banks could charge whatever customers were willing to pay. Now people all over the country receive letters in the mail with a Wilmington postmark from banks offering credit card applications and various banking and credit card opportunities.

But these opportunities pose a real problem. They come with hefty penalties, should customers be unable to pay on time. Delaware author Eric Zencey dislikes these laws that allowed businesses to tempt folks into making purchases so the credit-offering company can make money. He is angry at the suburban sprawl that has spoiled the natural environment and the prospect of big money brokers taking over his small, quiet state. He says, "In Delaware as elsewhere, the landscape made by law is fit for the typical modern consumer-worker, who is not so much a citizen or a townsman—but an atomized particle in a mass, a human who asks nothing more from an ecosystem than the opportunity to ignore it—to be sped on good roads from job to home to shopping, and in summer, on an occasional trip to the beach."

A second important change in state business law concerned taxes. In most states, banks pay one flat rate of income tax. Thanks to the FCDA, as a bank in Delaware earns more, its tax rate goes down.

Banking emerged as a major industry in Delaware during the early 1980s.

EARNING A LIVING

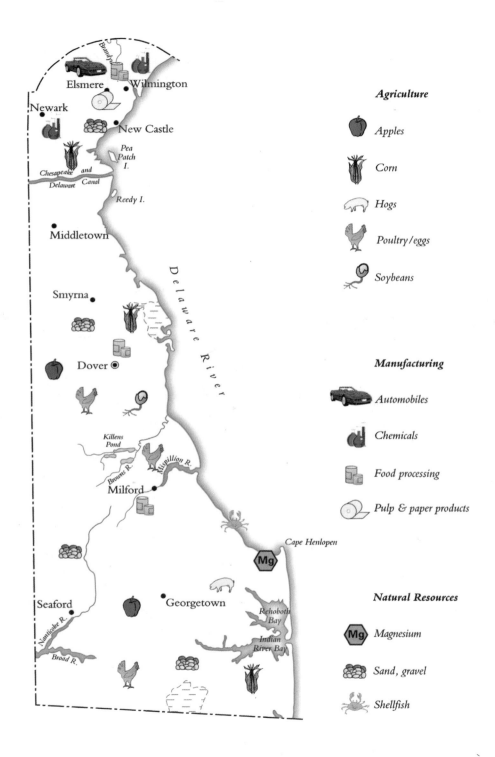

Elsmere
Wilmington
Brandy
Newark
New Castle
Pea Patch I.
Chesapeake and Delaware Canal
Reedy I.
Middletown
Delaware River
Smyrna
Dover
Killens Pond
Browns R.
Mispillion R.
Milford
Cape Henlopen
Mg
Seaford
Georgetown
Rehoboth Bay
Indian River Bay
Nanticoke R.
Broad R.

Agriculture

Apples

Corn

Hogs

Poultry/eggs

Soybeans

Manufacturing

Automobiles

Chemicals

Food processing

Pulp & paper products

Natural Resources

Mg Magnesium

Sand, gravel

Shellfish

This allowed the banks that charge high rates to consumers to benefit from the lower taxes resulting from increased bank profits. Once the FCDA became law, banks from across the nation flocked to Delaware to set up offices. Since then, banking has become a huge business in a state formerly known mainly for making chemicals.

BROILERS, BEACHES, AND SEAFOOD

Most banking and chemical businesses are based in and around Wilmington. The flat land of central and southern Delaware is prime farm country, yielding soybeans, corn, potatoes, dairy products, and poultry.

Poultry Farms

Delaware farmers raise 282.3 million broiler chickens. The broiler chicken industry, one of Delaware's biggest businesses, actually started by accident. One day in the early 1920s Cecile and Wilmer Steele, who lived near Ocean

One of Delaware's largest industries is raising poultry.

View, placed an order for fifty chicks. The Steeles were a farming couple who wanted to sell eggs to make a little extra money. By mistake, they received five hundred chicks, not fifty. Instead of returning the unordered chicks, the Steeles raised the whole shipment in a piano crate. About four months later, they sold the chicks for a huge profit. The next year they ordered one thousand chicks, and again they made a big profit. Competing farmers saw how the Steeles were making money and decided to raise large numbers of chickens, too. By the mid-1920s, the broiler industry in Sussex County was booming. It continues to be highly profitable today.

Fruits of the Sea

In 2004 commercial fishing accounted for $95.4 million of Delaware's state products. Until the 1950s, when a parasite in Delaware Bay ruined the business, oysters were the most sought-after catch in Delaware. Although some oysters are still harvested today, the people who work on Delaware's water are more likely to catch clams, fish, and crabs. Seafood lovers regard Delaware crabs as a true delicacy.

Delaware's seaside communities, such as Rehoboth Beach, Bethany Beach, and Dewey Beach, depend on tourists to occupy their sandy shorelines and spend money on food and lodging. So many visitors come from Washington, D.C., to Rehoboth Beach in the summer that the Delaware beach town has been nicknamed the Nation's Summer Capital.

The name *Rehoboth* is from a biblical word meaning "open spaces." That has become a bit of a joke on the Delaware seacoast, since more and more homes are being built there. Local folks like to see their area grow and prosper. But at the same time, they don't want their communities to lose their low-key feel. If too many people move in, the beach towns may become as congested as the cities newcomers wished to escape. The question is, How much development is too much?

Oysters were once found in abundance off Delaware's shores. Today, they are still harvested but in lesser quantities.

BORDER BATTLES

Through the years Delaware has battled with neighbors of common waterways. In 2007 a dispute erupted with New Jersey over who owns rights of access to the Delaware River. New Jersey wanted to build a modern natural gas storage and processing plant along the shoreline. But it needed to build a pier into the water for tankers to dock and unload.

Delaware objected, saying it owned access rights under a 1905 boundary settlement. That settlement said that each state owned access rights to its own shoreline. But a 1934 decision complicated the issue by declaring Delaware's ownership of its shoreline to the low-water area on the New Jersey side. This means that if Delaware chooses, it could block docking of any vessel on New Jersey shores. So far, judges have sided with Delaware in what has become a very complex affair.

MIXING UP THE ECONOMY

State government and transportation and utilities employ smaller but significant percentages of workers. The state hires scientists to manage wildlife refuges, including the Bombay Hook National Wildlife Refuge. In addition, a small mining industry contributes $21.8 million to Delaware's economy. The industry involves mining and processing of sand and gravel for the construction industry and magnesium compounds and gemstones.

The northern Delaware city of Newark is home to additional manufacturing and businesses. Automakers DaimlerChrysler and General Motors maintain assembly plants in Newark. The city houses the main campus of

19,000 students who attend the University of Delaware. One of the more unusual businesses in the state that is also located in Newark is W. L. Gore and Associates. This company makes Gore-Tex, a material used in everything from dental floss to guitar strings. Gore-Tex is best known for its use in outerwear donned by skiers, hunters, and backpackers. The company was founded in 1958 by a man named Bill Gore, who used to work at Du Pont.

Automobile manufacturing plants are found in Newark, Delaware.

To boost tourism, Delaware introduced gambling to the state. Here visitors play the slot machines at Dover Downs.

TOURISM, SLOT MACHINES, AND HORSES

Almost one in ten Delawareans work in the tourist industry. In recent years, Delaware has nurtured tourism as a way to bring income—and people—into the state. During the 1990s business leaders and lawmakers saw gambling as a good way to boost tourism. In 1996 the state added slot machine gambling to its many allowed gambling operations. The state's three racetracks installed slot machines on their grounds. Slots and horse racing existed alongside state-approved harness racing, bingo parlors, and a lottery.

Many of Delaware's leaders, including then-governor Thomas Carper, were against adding slot machines. Some were concerned that increased gambling opportunities would bring organized crime into the state. Others believed gambling was sinful. One overriding concern was whether or not casino gambling in Delaware could compete with the big-time gambling operations in Atlantic City, New Jersey, just a short drive away.

In response to these concerns, the state decided to permit casino gambling only at Delaware's three horse-racing tracks, where betting on horses was already legal. The racetracks had been doing poorly. They had not been attracting the best horses and were not living up to their potential as moneymakers. Gambling supporters thought that the addition of casino-type gambling would attract more customers and better quality horses.

So far the experiment has succeeded in raising money. The state receives roughly 35 percent of the tracks' profits from the casino gambling. Slots have been modernized for video lottery terminals, which have increased participation in the Delaware lottery. Race tracks have expanded to include hotels, restaurants, and casinos. Gambling has turned into big business in Delaware.

Chapter Six

Sightseeing and Sunbathing

For a small state, Delaware offers a host of activities and sights. From lavish mansions to relaxing beaches, Delaware can keep any sightseer busy.

HISTORIC WILMINGTON

Northern Delaware provides many cultural avenues. Mostly, the du Pont family is responsible for these cultural attractions. Many sites were once du Pont homes.

The king of Delaware mansions is Winterthur Museum and Gardens. The 60-acre estate is located 6 miles northwest of Wilmington. At one time, the home and gardens functioned as Henry Francis du Pont's country getaway.

The main building at Winterthur is nine stories high and contains 196 rooms. But the mansion was much smaller when it was first built. It grew because of Henry du Pont's hobby: collecting American antiques. He began

A visit to Delaware isn't complete without a trip to the beach.

The Winterthur Museum was once the country estate of Henry Francis du Pont.

by buying rare furniture. Then he purchased entire rooms full of early American furnishings. Within a short time, however, a major problem developed: he ran out of space for his treasures. To solve his problem, du Pont built additions to the house.

Today, Winterthur houses the world's largest collection of American decorative arts. Visitors can see such historical treasures as a dinner service made for George Washington, an entire room from Massachusetts dating to the 1600s, and silver tankards crafted by the famous patriot Paul Revere.

Winterthur's sights are not limited to the indoors. Outside are lush gardens and wooded paths where visitors can take relaxing strolls. On these grounds Winterthur hosts special events throughout the year. Among the biggest is a Sunday in May filled with horse races called Point-to-Point. The day's highlights are the steeplechase races, where horses jump over hedges and fences. There are also pony races and a parade of antique carriages.

The tranquil gardens of Winterthur Estate in Wilmington.

How did Winterthur get its unusual name? The mansion was originally built in 1839 by Evelina Gabrielle du Pont and her husband, James Antoine Bidermann. Bidermann named his new home for the city of Winterthur, Switzerland, where his ancestors had lived. When Henry Francis du Pont inherited the estate in 1927, he kept the name.

More Homes of the Rich and Famous

Henry Francis was not the only du Pont to leave a fascinating legacy to the people of Delaware. Another plush residence open to the public is Nemours Mansion and Gardens. The 102-room home on 300 acres of land is named for the du Pont family's ancestral home in France. Similar to Winterthur, Nemours main mansion houses priceless works of art, fine European tapestries, and antique furniture. The lush gardens provide an added bonus for

The formal gardens at the Nemours Mansion are considered the finest example of French style gardens in the United States.

visitors. Alfred I. du Pont, who built Nemours, based his gardens on the formal gardens that surround French palaces.

Another du Pont mansion, the Hagley Museum, is located just north of Wilmington. The estate offers more than just a museum. It hails as the place "where the du Pont story begins." Located in the woods high on the banks of Brandywine Creek, the grounds of Hagley Museum include the first du Pont mansion built by Éleuthère Irénée du Pont, founder of the family powder works. This mansion was built in 1803.

What makes Hagley different from other du Pont estates are the historic buildings on the grounds. Du Pont's original gunpowder mills are preserved there. An 1814 cotton mill shares the grounds with a working 1870s machine shop. At a spot called Blacksmith Hill, buildings show how mill

Historic buildings, such as this grain mill, still stand at the Hagley Museum.

workers lived 140 years ago. There's even a restored period school with attached wooden desks, rows of quill pens, and small slate chalkboards.

Beyond the Du Ponts

One of the oldest Protestant churches still in use in North America sits on the outskirts of downtown Wilmington. It is officially called Holy Trinity Episcopal Church, although locals refer to it as the Old Swedes Church. The stone church was built in 1698 by a Swedish congregation. Nearby is the Hendrickson House, a stone farmhouse built in 1690 in Pennsylvania but moved to this location.

Within walking distance of the Old Swedes Church is the Kalmar Nyckel Shipyard Museum. The *Kalmar Nyckel* was the boat that brought the first Swedish settlers to Delaware in 1638. The museum tells about that first landing along with the history of shipbuilding in the region. A replica of the *Kalmar Nyckel* sails up and down the Christina and Delaware rivers.

No tour of Wilmington is complete without a stop at Rodney Square. The downtown square was named in memory of the Delaware patriot who made a famous ride to Philadelphia in 1776. Caesar Rodney, a justice of the peace, rode 80 miles across Delaware to Philadelphia through thunder and rain to cast his vote for independence. He arrived on July 2, 1776, just before the vote took place. He has been quoted as saying, "As I believe the voice of my constituents and of all sensible and honest men is in favor of independence, and my own judgment concurs with them. I vote for independence." The statue of Rodney on horseback sits as a centerpiece of the square.

Wilmington also offers its share of quality museums. The Delaware Museum of Natural History houses more than one hundred displays, including dioramas of African animals and extinct birds in their natural habitats. Favorite exhibits include a re-creation of Australia's Great Barrier Reef and a massive shell collection.

A statue of Delaware patriot Caesar Rodney stands in Wilmington in Rodney Square.

The Delaware Art Museum is best known for its collection of American art, including works by painters Howard Pyle, Winslow Homer, and Maxfield Parrish. Other respected Wilmington museums are the Delaware History Museum, which is housed in a former Woolworth's department store.

IN AND AROUND NEW CASTLE

New Castle was once described in *American Heritage* magazine as possibly "the closest thing to a ghost town on the East coast." The comment refers to the fact that New Castle, a village of nearly five thousand people, is a beautifully preserved historic town. Although it sits just 2 miles south of the Delaware Memorial Bridge and busy Interstate 295, the town looks much as it did two hundred years ago. And people have lived in the same houses throughout New Castle's, and Delaware's, history.

Colonial brick homes are well preserved in New Castle.

Why is New Castle so well preserved? In the late 1700s, the town was an important stop on a stagecoach route connecting Philadelphia, Annapolis, and Baltimore. By the mid-1800s, however, Philadelphia and Baltimore grew into the region's biggest cities. New roads and railroad lines that bypassed New Castle were built to link those two major cities. Because New Castle was no longer an important stopping point for travelers, construction of new buildings declined. But luckily for tourists and historians, city leaders maintained New Castle's original buildings.

Most of the structures in New Castle are made from brick. One is the Old Court House, which was built in 1732. The four flags on the balcony are from Sweden, the Netherlands, Great Britain, and the United States, all nations that have governed New Castle at some point in history.

Along Third Street is a group of brick houses dating to Delaware's earliest days. The Old Dutch House is commonly referred to as the Amstel House. It was built in the 1730s as a small home with a steeply pitched roof and detailed woodwork by the town's wealthy landowner, Dr. John Fihney. This modest house is the oldest in New Castle, and it is believed to be the oldest in the entire state. The house's history involves many of the town's prominent and colorful families. George Washington attended a wedding in the parlor.

Probably Delaware's most significant historic building outside Wilmington is in Fort Delaware State Park. The park is located on Pea Patch Island in the Delaware River. The only way to get there is by boat. A fort on the island housed Confederate prisoners of war during the Civil War. This five-sided structure has huge, solid granite walls surrounded by a moat. Despite the massive walls and moat, some prisoners escaped and were sheltered by supporters of the Confederacy in Delaware and Maryland.

Pea Patch Island is the home to Fort Delaware.

At one time, people risked their lives to escape the fort, but today they pay to visit it. Inside are exhibits relating to the Civil War. Travelers also come to Pea Patch Island to walk its many nature trails. Wading birds, such as herons and egrets, find the island an inviting place to make their nests. An observation tower helps visitors spot the birds. Some people enjoy a boat ride around Pea Patch Island. Sunset cruises are offered on summer evenings.

DELAWARE'S WILD SIDE

Not every site in northern Delaware is about history. Lums Pond State Park, located just above the canal, is built around the largest freshwater pond in the state. It is an ideal spot for boaters to rent sailboats, rowboats, pedal boats, and canoes. One of the park's unusual features is the Sensory Trail, which encourages walkers to use all their senses rather than just sight. There are also trails for biking, horseback riding, hiking, and snowmobiling.

TEN LARGEST CITIES

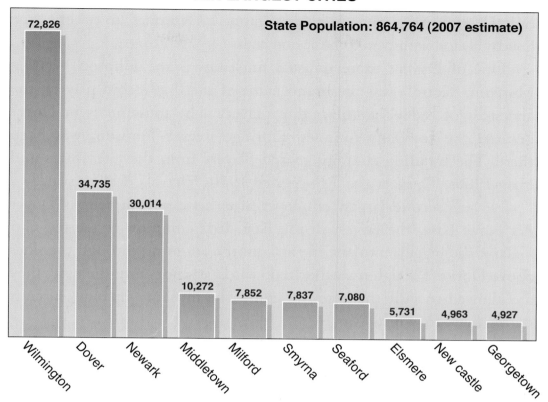

State Population: 864,764 (2007 estimate)

- Wilmington — 72,826
- Dover — 34,735
- Newark — 30,014
- Middletown — 10,272
- Milford — 7,852
- Smyrna — 7,837
- Seaford — 7,080
- Elsmere — 5,731
- New castle — 4,963
- Georgetown — 4,927

Fox Point State Park is a newly developed park tucked amid the buildings and highways of the Wilmington metropolitan area. Located along the banks of the Delaware River, the park lures people wanting a green and open place to ride their bicycles, have a picnic, or play a game of horseshoes.

CAPITAL ATTRACTIONS

The state capital, Dover, is home to some noted museums. The Delaware Agricultural Museum and Village, a living old-fashioned community, houses a collection of old tractors and farm tools and an old barbershop, one-room schoolhouse, store, and train station from the late 1800s. Every early December the museum holds a "farmer's Christmas" to celebrate the holiday season with period music and crafts.

One of Dover's more unusual museums is the Johnson Victrola Museum. Victrola was the brand name of the first record players, the ancestors of today's compact disc players. The museum is in Dover because the company founder, Eldridge Reeves Johnson, was born there. The building contains record players from the late 1800s and early 1900s. There is also a re-created 1920s Victrola dealer's store.

Dover's second-largest employer after state government is Dover Air Force Base, the largest in the East. It is common to see the C-5 Galaxy, the biggest airplane in the country, zooming through the skies above Dover. Though unauthorized visitors cannot enter the base, they are allowed to visit the base museum. The museum includes aircraft dating back to World War II.

Dover residents who want to cool off sometimes head south to Killens Pond State Park, which sports a water park complete with water slides and pools. Those searching for more peaceful activities can take a narrated pontoon boat tour of Killens Pond. The park's hiking trails cover Ice Storm Trail, which gives visitors a chance to observe the forest's recovery from harsh ice storms that hit the park in 1994.

Visitors can discover military planes at the Dover Air Force Base.

HONORING A LOCAL BASEBALL STAR

From the 1880s until 1947, African Americans were not allowed to join Major League Baseball teams. So blacks formed their own organizations, known as the Negro Leagues. The Negro Leagues produced some of the most talented ballplayers anywhere. Star third-baseman, William Julius "Judy" Johnson, was one of those players.

In 1975 Judy Johnson was inducted into the National Baseball Hall of Fame in Cooperstown, New York. He was credited with being one of the greatest third basemen in the history of the Negro Leagues. Johnson played from 1920 until 1935 with the Philadelphia Hilldales, the Homestead Grays, and the Pittsburgh Crawfords. A clutch hitter and quick fielder, Johnson led the Hilldales to three straight pennants from 1923 through

1925. During those years he maintained batting averages of .391, .369, and .392. His playing career over, Johnson became a coach and scout with the Philadelphia Athletics and the Philadelphia Phillies.

After the long-time Wilmington resident died in 1989, city leaders searched for a way to honor their local hero. In 1993 the Judy Johnson Field at Daniel S. Frawley Stadium opened as home of the Wilmington Blue Rocks. Three years later, the Judy Johnson Memorial Foundation began sponsoring the annual Judy Johnson Night—A Tribute to Negro League Baseball to honor other former players of the Negro Leagues.

PLACES TO SEE

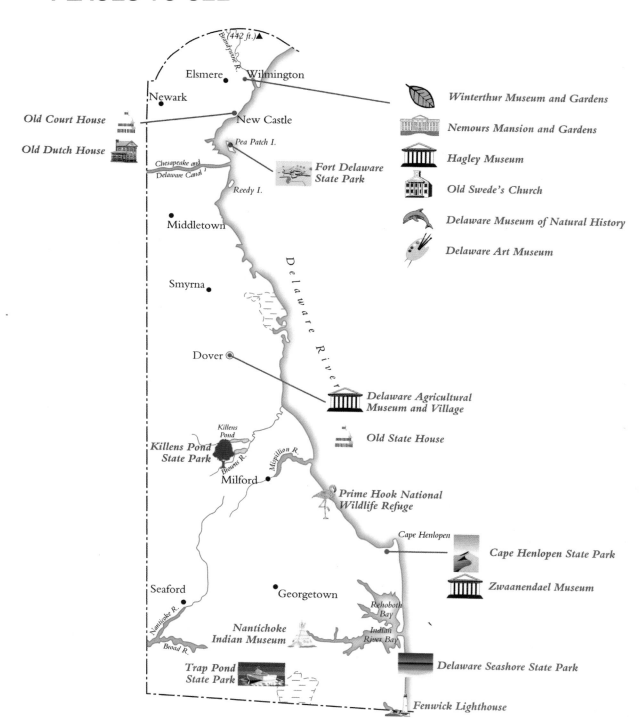

(442 ft.) ▲

Brandywine R.

Elsmere   Wilmington

Newark

Winterthur Museum and Gardens

Old Court House

Nemours Mansion and Gardens

New Castle

Old Dutch House

Hagley Museum

Pea Patch I.

Old Swede's Church

Chesapeake and
Delaware Canal

Fort Delaware
State Park

Delaware Museum of Natural History

Reedy I.

Delaware Art Museum

Middletown

Delaware River

Smyrna

Dover

Delaware Agricultural
Museum and Village

Killens
Pond

Old State House

Killens Pond
State Park

Browns R.

Mispillion R.

Milford

Prime Hook National
Wildlife Refuge

Cape Henlopen

Cape Henlopen State Park

Seaford

Georgetown

Rehoboth
Bay

Zwaanendael Museum

Nanticoke R.

Nantichoke
Indian Museum

Indian
River Bay

Broad R.

Trap Pond
State Park

Delaware Seashore State Park

Fenwick Lighthouse

RELAXING IN DELAWARE

Southern Delaware is the vacation destination for people who want a rest from their work or school grind. There beach resorts rule for those who wish to do nothing more than stretch out on the sand and relax.

The busiest beach town is Rehoboth Beach, a seaside setting first developed in 1873 by Methodist church leaders. The Methodists were looking for a quiet place to hold religious summer camp meetings. Today, Rehoboth Beach is less than quiet, especially in summer. The community's winter population is a little over 1,200. But on a hot summer day, the population of the area can swell to 50,000. Aside from the sun and sand, tourists admire the town's many hundred-year-old homes on tree-lined streets.

Thousands wait in anticipation for a seaside fireworks display in Rehoboth.

Farther south near the Maryland border are Bethany Beach and Fenwick Island. The Delaware travel industry promotes these places as "quiet resorts." The resorts don't have large hotels like those found at Rehoboth Beach. Both are mainly residential, where people buy their places to stay. Delaware Secretary of Agriculture Jack Tarburton bought a vacation home in this part of the state. What he says he loves best is "the solitude—the only commerce in town is one phone booth, and the scenery changes every day."

Delaware's northernmost beach resort is the town of Lewes, which hugs the eastern edge of Cape Henlopen. Lewes offers proof that even at the beach, Delaware visitors cannot escape history. Near here in 1631, the Dutch founded the settlement they called Zwaanendael. Today, visitors can explore the Zwaanendael Museum, a replica of a Dutch town hall. Inside are military and maritime relics and the remains of a Dutch ship that sank in 1798.

Like New Castle, Lewes has a collection of preserved old buildings open to visitors. The buildings include a nineteenth-century country store and an 1850 doctor's office. Aside from history and beaches, Lewes is also known for its fine boutique and antique shopping.

Visitors can stretch their legs at Cape Henlopen State Park, home of the highest sand dune between Cape Cod in Massachusetts and Cape Hatteras in North Carolina. Known as the Great Dune, the Henlopen rises 80 feet above the coastline. People can also exercise their legs by climbing the observation tower built during World War II. The tower served as a lookout post to spot possible enemy attacks. During the war, a German submarine was captured off the coast of Delaware and New Jersey. Today, visitors who trudge up the 115 steps to the top are rewarded with a spectacular view.

Lewes is a historic seaside town in Delaware.

ECOTOURISM IN DELAWARE

A current trend in travel is ecotourism, which is short for "ecology tourism." This is travel based on experiencing nature and helping the environment.

A visitors' guide to southern Delaware describes the difference between a tourist and an eco-traveler: "A tourist sits on the beach all day hoping for a suntan. An eco-traveler walks the beach in search of clues to Delaware's marine environment. He or she may take a guided tour, participate in a sea-going classroom activity or stalk the salt marshes for a glimpse of a rare bird."

Many people think that ecotourism takes place mainly in national parks or in the rain forests of tropical countries. But Delaware is filled with opportunities for the ecotourist. Since the state sits along the Atlantic flyway, migrating birds fly by or stop. The best time for bird-watching is spring and early summer, when horseshoe crabs lay their eggs on the beach. For shorebirds, the eggs are like ice cream to a kid.

Every October, the University of Delaware hosts a Coastal Clean-Up and Coast Day near Lewes. Other ecotourist activities include canoeing down the Nanticoke River and observing whales and dolphin. Visitors who take part in activities such as these leave with more than a suntan. They gain a deeper understanding of Delaware's wildlife and natural resources.

Another area for outdoor fun in the southern reaches of the state is Trap Pond State Park. Outdoors people can go boating among the bald cypress trees. Some might wish to paddle a canoe or stroll the trails at Prime Hook National Wildlife Refuge, a haven for Delaware's birds and other animals.

Southern Delaware is home to the Nanticoke Indians, who mostly live near Millsboro. They keep their traditions alive at the Nanticoke Indian Museum, located in a restored schoolhouse. The museum displays American-Indian pottery, beadwork, baskets, ancient arrowheads, and other objects.

Delaware offers a wealth of treasures from American-Indian artifacts to historic mansions to amazing natural wonders. Visitors can explore the nooks and crannies and open spaces of the state by bicycle, car, or train. There are interesting people to meet and places to go within the First State's narrow borders.

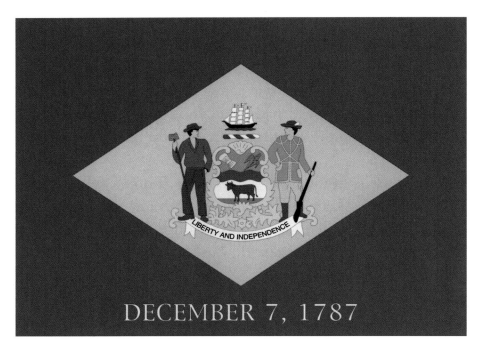

THE FLAG: Delaware's flag depicts the image from the state seal inside a buff-colored diamond against a blue background. December 7, 1787, the date Delaware became the first state, appears below the diamond. The flag was adopted in 1913.

THE SEAL: In the middle of the state seal, which was introduced in 1777, a farmer and a soldier support a shield. The shield shows corn, wheat, and an ox, all of which symbolize agriculture. Above the shield is a sailing ship, representing New Castle County's shipbuilding industry.

State Survey

Statehood: December 7, 1787

Origin of Name: From Delaware Bay, which was named in honor of Lord De La Warr, the governor of the Virginia Colony

Nickname: First State

Capital: Dover

Motto: Liberty and Independence

Bird: Blue hen chicken

Flower: Peach blossom

Tree: American holly

Fish: Weakfish

Bug: Ladybug

Mineral: Sillimanite

Colors: Colonial blue and buff

Peach blossoms

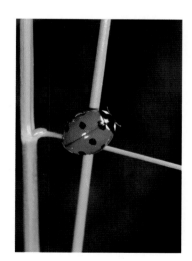

Ladybug

OUR DELAWARE

The official song of the First State was adopted by the state legislature in 1925.

Words by Geo. B. Hynson　　　　　　　**Music by Will. M.S. Brown**

Oh, our Del - a - ware! Our be - lov - ed Del - a - ware! For the

sun is shin - ing o - ver our be - lov - ed Del - a - ware.

Oh! our Del - a - ware! Our be - lov - ed Del - a - ware! Here's the

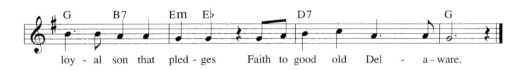

loy - al son that pled - ges Faith to good old Del - a - ware.

GEOGRAPHY

Highest Point: 442 feet above sea level, on Ebright Road in New Castle County

Lowest Point: sea level along the coast

Area: 2,026 square miles

Greatest Distance North to South: 96 miles

Greatest Distance East to West: 35 miles

Bordering States: New Jersey to the east, Pennsylvania to the north, Maryland to the south and west

Hottest Recorded Temperature: 110 °F in Millsboro on July 21, 1930

Coldest Recorded Temperature: −17 °F in Millsboro on January 17, 1893

Average Annual Precipitation: 45 inches

Major Rivers: Brandywine, Broadkill, Christina, Delaware, Indian, Mispillion, Murderkill, Nanticoke, Smyrna, St. Jones

Major Lakes: Hoopes, Lums, Noxontown, Red Mill, Silver

Trees: bald cypress, beech, black tupelo, hickory, holly, loblolly pine, magnolia, oak, sassafras, sweet gum

Wild Plants: azalea, blueberry, cranberry, crocus, floating heart, hibiscus, honeysuckle, lady's slipper, violet, water lily

Animals: beaver, deer, gray fox, mink, muskrat, otter, rabbit, red fox, snapping turtle

Birds: blue heron, cardinal, duck, finch, grackle, hawk, oriole, sandpiper, snowy egret, teal, woodpecker, wren

Fish: bass, carp, catfish, clam, eel, oyster, porgie, rockfish, shad, trout, white perch

Endangered Animals: American peregrine falcon, bald eagle, bog turtle, Delmarva Peninsula fox squirrel, piping plover

Endangered Plants: Canby's dropwort, Knieskern's beaked rush, small whorled pogonia, swamp pink

TIMELINE

Delaware History

1500s The Lenni-Lenape and Nanticoke Indians live in present-day Delaware.

1609 Englishman Henry Hudson enters Delaware Bay while sailing for the Dutch, becoming the first European to visit the region.

1610 Samuel Argall of the Virginia Colony visits the bay and names it De La Warr Bay after Virginia's governor.

Piping Plover

1631 The Dutch found Delaware's first European settlement, Zwaanen-dael, at present-day Lewes, but it is destroyed within a year.

1638 Swedish colonists found Fort Christina, Delaware's first permanent European settlement.

1652 The Dutch take control of the region.

1664 England seizes control of Delaware.

1682 William Penn receives Delaware territory as part of Pennsylvania.

1704 Delaware's first legislature, separate from Pennsylvania's, meets.

1754 Delaware's first library is established in Wilmington.

1769 Newark Academy, which will later become the University of Delaware, is founded.

1775 The American Revolution begins.

1777 Dover becomes Delaware's capital.

1785 Delaware's first successful newspaper, the *Delaware Gazette*, begins publication.

1787 Delaware becomes the first state to ratify the U.S. Constitution.

1802 Éleuthère Irénée du Pont establishes a powder mill on the banks of Brandywine Creek, marking the beginning of the du Pont empire.

1829 The Chesapeake and Delaware Canal opens: Delaware establishes a system of public schools.

1861–1865 Delaware fights for the Union during the Civil War.

1897 Delaware adopts its fourth and present constitution.

1907 The Du Pont Company is sued under the Sherman Anti-Trust Act. It is eventually forced to give up much of its explosives business.

1917–1918 About 10,000 Delawareans fight in World War I.

1922 Delaware's first radio station, WDEL, begins broadcasting in Wilmington.

1938 The Du Pont Company develops nylon.

1939–1945 World War II.

1951 The Delaware Memorial Bridge opens across the Delaware River, connecting Delaware and New Jersey.

1963 Delaware bans segregation in public places.

1969 Bill to end housing discrimination passes.

1971 The state legislature passes the Coastal Zone Act, banning construction of industrial plants along the state's coastline.

1981 Delaware enacts the Financial Center Development Act, which encourages out-of-state banks to move some of their operations to Delaware.

1987 Delaware celebrates its 200th birthday.

1995 Route 1 bridge over the Chesapeake and Delaware Canal opens.

1996 The federal government recognizes the Delaware Indian tribe.

2000 Ruth Ann Minner is elected Delaware's first woman governor.

2002 Clean Air Act passes, banning smoking in public places.

2007 Border dispute erupts between Delaware and New Jersey over shoreline rights over a proposal by New Jersey to build a natural gas storage and processing plant.

ECONOMY

Agricultural Products: apples, cattle, corn, greenhouse and nursery products, hay, hogs, potatoes, poultry, soybeans

Manufactured Products: apparel, chemicals, food products, luggage, medical supplies, nylon, transportation equipment

Apples

Natural Resources: granite, magnesium, sand and gravel, shellfish

Business and Trade: banking, insurance, real estate, tourism, wholesale and retail trade

CALENDAR OF CELEBRATIONS

Great Delaware Kite Festival Hundreds of colorful kites soar high in the sky at this event marking the beginning of spring. It takes place the Friday before Easter at Cape Henlopen State Park near Lewes.

Wilmington Garden Day Many lovely gardens and houses in the Wilmington area are open for touring on the first Saturday in May.

Old Dover Days Dover celebrates its rich history each May with crafts exhibits and tours of historic homes.

Italian Festival Each June, 300,000 people descend on Wilmington to feast on rich Italian food such as spezzato, cannoli, and muffuletta while Italian music wafts through the air. A carnival and fireworks display add to the fun.

Separation Day In June, New Castle marks Delaware's declaration of independence from Great Britain with music, fireworks, and a parade of boats.

Old-Fashioned Ice Cream Festival Sampling as many flavors of ice cream as possible is the centerpiece of this July event in Wilmington. Other activities, such as demonstrations of old-fashioned hand-cranked organs, re-create the atmosphere of a festival in the late 1800s.

Delaware State Fair Each July in Harrington, Delaware hosts an old-fashioned state fair, complete with livestock competitions, carnival rides, games, concerts, delicious homemade breads, jams, and other treats, and a variety of other fun activities.

Delaware State Fair

Nanticoke Indian Powwow American Indians from up and down the East Coast travel to Millsboro in September for this celebration of American-Indian culture. The event includes ceremonial dances, storytelling, and Indian foods and crafts.

Delaware Nature Society Harvest Moon Festival Hayrides, pony rides, freshly pressed cider, nature walks, music, games, and arts and crafts are all part of this traditional October event in Greenville.

Punkin Chunkin World Championship Begun in 1986 near Bridgeville, this three-day contest involves launching pumpkins into the air with machines and attracts 20,000 visitors.

Coast Day Each October the University of Delaware in Lewes opens its facilities and research ship to the public. Films, demonstrations, and exhibits all help educate visitors about Delaware's coastal environment.

Sea Witch Halloween and Fiddlers Festival Rehoboth Beach cuts loose for this fun-filled festival of all things spooky in October. You can tiptoe through a haunted house, relax on a horse-drawn hayride, and watch an antique car show. You'll surely want to participate in the wild costume contest—there's also one for your pet—and maybe even the broom-tossing contest.

Yuletide at Winterthur During the holiday season, several of this Wilmington mansion's rooms are decked out in traditional holiday decorations.

Sea Witch Halloween Festival

Richard Allen (1760–1831) founded the African Methodist Episcopal Church, the first black religious denomination in the United States. Allen was born a slave in Philadelphia and grew up on a plantation in Delaware. He eventually bought his freedom and became a Methodist minister. Allen ultimately concluded that because of racism, blacks needed to form their own churches. As a result, in 1816 he established the African Methodist Episcopal Church.

Henry Seidel Canby (1878–1961) was an editor who played an important role in increasing the number of people who read American literature. Canby was the first professor at Yale University to specialize in American literature. Later, he founded the *Saturday Review of Literature*, the leading literary weekly of the 1920s and 1930s. He was also the first chairman of the board of the Book-of-the-Month Club. Canby grew up in Wilmington.

Annie Jump Cannon (1863–1941), a native of Dover, developed a system for classifying stars. While working at Harvard College Observatory, she used this system to catalog 350,000 stars and other heavenly bodies. She is credited with discovering hundreds of stars. Cannon was the first woman to receive an honorary doctorate from Oxford University in England.

Wallace Hume Carothers (1896–1937) was a chemist who developed nylon while working for Delaware's Du Pont Company. Carothers, a native of Iowa, earned his Ph.D. in 1924 and soon began teaching chemistry at Harvard. In 1928, because of his reputation as a brilliant

Wallace Hume Carothers

researcher, du Pont hired him to head its research program. His work there led to the production of the world's first synthetic fiber, nylon.

Felix Darley (1822–1888) was the leading book illustrator of his time. From the 1840s until his death, any book that said "illustrated by Darley" was automatically a big seller. During his career, he illustrated such classics as Washington Irving's *Legend of Sleepy Hollow* and James Fenimore Cooper's *The Deerslayer*. Darley was born in Philadelphia and moved to Claymont, Delaware, after he married.

Éleuthère Irénée du Pont (1771–1834) launched one of America's most successful business empires when he founded a gunpowder mill on the banks of the Brandywine River near Wilmington. Du Pont was born into a wealthy family in Paris and immigrated to the United States in 1799.

Oliver Evans (1755–1819) was an inventor born in Newport, Delaware. As a young man working in a flour mill, he invented the grain elevator and developed other milling machinery, creating a fully automated mill that could be run by just one person. This vastly improved the milling process, which until then had been powered by waterwheels. Evans also built one of the first high-pressure steam engines and invented what was likely America's first self-propelled vehicle for ground travel.

Thomas Garrett (1789–1871) was a leading abolitionist in Wilmington, who helped 2,700 people escape slavery. Garrett's house in Wilmington was an important refuge for slaves fleeing north on the Underground Railroad. In 1848 Garrett was convicted of helping slaves escape and had to sell all his property to pay the fine.

Dallas Green (1934–   ), a baseball manager, led the Philadelphia Phillies to a World Series victory in 1980. Green began his career as a pitcher with the Phillies in the early 1960s. He later managed some Phillie farm clubs before becoming manager of the major league team in 1979. Green has also worked for the Chicago Cubs, the New York Yankees, and the New York Mets. He was born in Newport.

Henry Heimlich (1920–   ) is a doctor who gained fame for developing the Heimlich maneuver, a method of preventing a person from choking to death. Through the 1960s, choking was a leading cause of accidental death in the United States. Heimlich realized that if a patient was squeezed, air would be forced out of his or her lungs. This often dislodged the object on which the person was choking. Heimlich published a study on the maneuver in 1974, and lives were saved by those who adopted it. Both Heimlich and his maneuver became well known. In the following years, the number of deaths from choking dropped dramatically. Heimlich was born in Wilmington.

Henry Heimlich

Eldridge Reeves Johnson (1867–1945) was a Wilmington native who made records and record players affordable to the average American. In 1901 Johnson founded the Victor Talking Machine Company. He soon developed a way of improving the sound quality of recorded discs and designed a machine that could duplicate the records more easily. The next year he produced more than a million discs. His company eventually became the Radio Corporation of America, or RCA.

William Julius "Judy" Johnson (1899–1989), a star third baseman in the Negro Leagues, was born in Wilmington. Johnson was a great hitter, with an estimated lifetime batting average of .344. After he retired, he worked as a scout for the Atlanta Braves and the Philadelphia Phillies, bringing many young black players to the major leagues. Johnson was inducted into the National Baseball Hall of Fame in 1975.

Thomas Macdonough (1783–1825) was a naval hero who was born in the Trap, which is now called Macdonough. He earned the nickname Hero of Lake Champlain after his American troops captured the entire British fleet in the Battle of Plattsburgh during the War of 1812.

Daniel Nathans (1928–   ) shared the 1978 Nobel Prize in Medicine for his research in genetics. Nathans's work on restriction enzymes paved the way for the development of artificial hormones. Nathans was born in Wilmington.

Howard Pyle (1853–1911), who was born in Wilmington, was an illustrator, famed for his bold lines and fertile imagination. His work published in *Harper's Weekly* established his reputation. He later created classic illustrations for such books as *The Merry Adventures of Robin Hood*. Pyle was also an influential teacher, helping develop the talents of such artists as Maxfield Parrish and N. C. Wyeth. After teaching elsewhere, in 1900 he founded the Howard Pyle School of Art in Wilmington, which provided illustration classes free of charge.

Jay Saunders Redding (1906–1988), a native of Wilmington, was an important literary critic and historian. His first book, *To Make a Poet Black*, published in 1939, was the first serious work about early African-American literature written by an African American. One of his most highly regarded books was *No Day of Triumph*, an angry, honest work that mixes autobiography with a discussion of black life in the South.

Estelle Taylor (1899–1958) was a beautiful movie star of the era of silent films. She appeared in such classics as *The Ten Commandments* and *Don Juan*. For a time she was married to boxer Jack Dempsey. Taylor was born in Wilmington.

George Thorogood (1951–   ), a blues-rock musician from Wilmington, has attracted legions of fans through his exuberant live shows. Thorogood and his band, the Destroyers, have had such hits as "Bad to the Bone" and "Move It On Over."

George Thorogood

TOUR THE STATE

Fort Delaware State Park (Delaware City) This fort, located on Pea Patch Island in the Delaware River, housed Confederate prisoners during the Civil War. Today, you can tour the dark cells where the prisoners were held. On a brighter note, the park also includes nature trails and a lively colony of shorebirds.

Old Dutch House (New Castle) Likely the oldest dwelling in Delaware, this house is furnished as it would have been in Dutch colonial times.

Bombay Hook National Wildlife Refuge (Smyrna) Rails and observation towers make this an excellent place to spot wildlife. The refuge is home to bald eagles, deer, shorebirds, and other creatures. The best times to visit are spring and fall, when thousands of migrating duck, snow geese, and other waterfowl stop there to feed.

Delaware Art Museum (Wilmington) This museum has a fine collection of paintings by American artists such as Winslow Homer and Edward Hopper.

Old Swedes Church (Wilmington) Built in 1698, this is one of the oldest churches in the United States. It is renowned for its beautiful black walnut pulpit.

Hagley Museum (Wilmington) At this site, you can visit the powder mill that was the beginning of the du Pont empire, along with later factories, the first du Pont mansion in Delaware, and a collection of antique wagons.

Hagley Museum

Nemours Mansion (Wilmington) This sprawling du Pont mansion, built in 1910, was modeled after the family estate in France. This 300-acre estate is famous for its formal garden.

Winterthur (Wilmington) Another du Pont house, Winterthur, grew from a 12-room residence to a gigantic museum that houses the nation's finest collection of early American decorative arts. Each of its nearly two hundred rooms displays a specific decorative style.

Corbit-Sharp House (Odessa) This beautifully preserved home was built in 1772. Much of the furniture in it belonged to the original owners.

Delaware Agricultural Museum and Village (Dover) Besides admiring antique farm equipment, you can visit an old-time barbershop, school-house, sawmill, blacksmith shop, and other historic buildings.

Old State House (Dover) Constructed in 1792, this is the second-oldest statehouse in continuous use in the United States. You can tour the restored chambers and view historical artifacts.

Johnson Victrola Museum (Dover) Step back in time at this museum, which looks like a music store from the 1920s. Windup record players, early jukeboxes, and old recordings document the early history of recorded music.

Air Mobility Command Museum (Dover) Vintage aircraft is on display at this museum on the Dover Air Force Base. The best time to visit is during open-house days, when kids can climb into the cockpit of the C-5 Galaxy, the largest American aircraft.

Delaware Seashore State Park (Rehoboth Beach) This peaceful site on Rehoboth Bay allows both ocean and bay swimming. It's also an ideal spot for fishing, clamming, surfing, and sunbathing.

Fenwick Island Lighthouse (Fenwick Island) This historic lighthouse has been warning ships off the shore since 1859.

Nanticoke Indian Museum (Millsboro) Ancient tools, weapons, and other artifacts educate visitors about how Delaware's Native Americans once lived.

Trap Pond State Park (Laurel) With both swampland and a large pond, this park is the perfect place to hike, bike, canoe, and picnic. During a visit to the park, you might see magnificent bald cypress trees, dazzling wildflowers, and a whole array of birds, from hummingbirds to great blue herons.

Cape Henlopen State Park (Lewes) Beautiful beaches and the biggest sand dunes in the Mid-Atlantic region are the highlights of this park.

FUN FACTS

Delaware became the first state on December 7, 1787, when it led the thirteen original states in ratifying the U.S. Constitution.

The first beauty contest in the United States was held in Rehoboth Beach in 1880. One of the three judges was the renowned inventor Thomas Edison.

Cape Henlopen State Park

Nylon was invented by researchers at the Du Pont Company in 1938.

The Delaware-Maryland border passes through the towns of Marydel and Delmar, both of which got their names by combining parts of the two state names.

Because of Delaware's business-friendly laws, more than half of the nation's five hundred largest corporations are officially incorporated there, even though they carry on virtually none of their business in the state.

Find Out More

Do you want to learn more about Delaware? Here are some suggestions for places to start.

BOOKS ABOUT DELAWARE PEOPLE, PLACES, AND HISTORY

Bial, Raymond. *The Delaware* (Lifeways). New York: Marshall Cavendish Benchmark, 2005.

Cheripko, Jan. *Caesar Rodney's Ride: The Story of an American Patriot.* Honesdale, PA: Boyds Mills Press, 2004.

DuBois, Muriel. *The Delaware Colony.* Mankato, MN: Capstone Press, 2005.

Hossell, Karen. *Delaware, 1638–1776* (Voices from Colonial America). Washington, D.C.: National Geographic Society, 2006.

Wiener, Roberta. *Delaware* (13 Colonies). Chicago: Raintree, 2005.

Worth, Richard. *Life in the Thirteen Colonies: Delaware.* Danbury, CT: Children's Press, 2004.

Yorinks, Adrienne. *Quilt of States: Piecing Together America.* Washington, D.C.: National Geographic, 2005.

DVD

Delaware, Bennett-Watt Media, www.bennett-watt.com/prodinfo.asp?
number=DVDDADE

WEB SITES

Delaware.gov-Kids Page

www.delaware.gov/egov/portal.nsf/portal/kids

This Web site provides information about Delaware from state facts and
maps to ghost stories and homework help.

Delaware Tribe of Indians

www.delawaretribeofindians.nsn.us

This site offers an overview and history of the Delaware Indian nation.

Historical Society of Delaware-Grandma's Attic Kid's Museum

www.hsd.org/hsdkids.htm

This special site for kids within the Delaware History Museum Online gives
the who, what, when, where, and general facts about Delaware and the people who developed the state.

State of Delaware home page

www.state.de.us

This site covers the range of activities important to Delaware's history and
making the state run today. Information covers current events, government,
economy, education, cultural events, and facts about the current governor.

Visit Delaware

www.visitdelaware.com

This site lists the fun stuff. Every day Delaware citizens and visitors
can learn about tours, art events, sports and recreation, and the best
places to shop.

Index

Page numbers in **boldface** are illustrations and charts.

ABOUT THE AUTHORS

Michael Schuman has written a dozen books for young people, as well as eight travel guides. His articles have appeared in the travel sections of more than one hundred newspapers in the United States and Canada and in several magazines. His travels have taken him to Delaware on many occasions.

Marlee Richards is an award-winning author of more than sixty-five books for readers of all ages. She writes about many different topics from history and biography to tooth fairies, raising kids, and the Pony Express. Her favorite topics allow her to play detective to find new and interesting facts for her readers. With the state series, she contacted people from the state to interview and investigated new regions of the country.